U.S.NRC
United States Nuclear Regulatory Commission
Protecting People and the Environment

FY 2013
CONGRESSIONAL
BUDGET
JUSTIFICATION

FY 2013
CONGRESSIONAL
BUDGET
JUSTIFICATION

TABLE OF
CONTENTS

TABLE OF CONTENTS

CONTENTS

TABLES

FIGURES

EXECUTIVE SUMMARY

EXECUTIVE SUMMARY

The U.S. Nuclear Regulatory Commission (NRC) is an independent Federal agency established to license and regulate the Nation's civilian use of byproduct, source, and special nuclear materials (SNM) to ensure adequate protection of public health and safety, promote the common defense and security, and protect the environment. The NRC has formulated its Fiscal Year (FY) 2013 Congressional Budget Justification to support the agency's Safety and Security strategic goals and objectives.

The NRC's Safety goal is to ensure adequate protection of public health and safety and the environment. The agency's safety program outcomes are to prevent the occurrence of any nuclear reactor accidents, inadvertent criticality events, acute radiation exposures, or significant releases of radioactive materials. The Security goal is to ensure the secure use and management of radioactive materials. The security program outcomes are to prevent any instances where licensed radioactive materials are used in a hostile manner in the United States.

The NRC continues to perform the critical functions to ensure the safe and secure use of byproduct, source, and SNM in the United States and to protect both the public and workers from radiation hazards that could result from the use of radioactive materials. The NRC's principal regulatory functions are to establish regulatory requirements and conduct confirmatory research to support requirements; issue licenses to facility owners, possessors, and users of nuclear materials; inspect these licensees to ensure they are in compliance with NRC requirements and operate safely and securely; and take appropriate enforcement action for violations of regulatory requirements.

THE MISSION OF THE U.S. NUCLEAR REGULATORY COMMISSION

License and regulate the Nation's civilian use of byproduct, source, and special nuclear materials to ensure adequate protection of public health and safety, promote the common defense and security, and protect the environment.

Following the Fukushima Daiichi accident, the NRC established a task force to conduct a systematic and methodical review of NRC's processes and regulations to determine whether the agency should make additional improvements to its regulatory system and to make recommendations to the Commission for its policy direction. The task force concluded that a sequence of events like the Fukushima accident is unlikely to occur in the United States and some appropriate measures have been implemented, reducing the likelihood of core damage and radiological releases. Therefore, continued

The Commission (left to right): Commissioner William D. Magwood, IV, Commissioner Kristine L. Svinicki, Chairman Gregory B. Jaczko, Commissioner George Apostolakis, Commissioner William C. Ostendorff.

operation and licensing activities do not pose an imminent risk to the public health and safety. However, the task force identified near-term actions that the agency should consider to enhance safety. Additionally, the Commission directed the task force to identify a framework and topics for review and assessment for a longer-term effort. In FY 2013, the NRC will conduct Commission-approved activities associated with the near-term recommendations, as well as safety improvements that are identified as part of the longer term effort.

At the time this budget was submitted, the Commission was considering the staffs proposed prioritization of the Fukushima Near-Term Task Force recommendations and regulatory actions to be taken in response to the events at Fukushima Daiichi. The NRC will ensure that regulatory changes necessary to maintain continued safety of the domestic nuclear energy will be accommodated and executed.

The NRC regulates every aspect of the civilian use of nuclear materials, from the processing of the uranium ore to the disposal of radioactive waste. This includes all of the steps and the facilities involved in the nuclear fuel cycle: extraction of the uranium from ore, conversion of the uranium into a form suitable for enrichment, enrichment of the uranium to a level and type suitable for nuclear fuel, and fabrication of the enriched uranium into fuel assemblies for use in reactors. The fuel assemblies are used in nuclear reactors and, when no longer efficient for reactor operations, are removed and stored as waste.

Since October 2007, the NRC has received 18 combined applications (including Watts Bar 2) to construct and operate new nuclear power reactors. Five different reactor designs are referenced in these applications; the NRC is currently reviewing the design applications for certification. These design certifications (DCs) will reduce the time required to approve a power reactor license application when a previously certified reactor design is used. If and when new power reactors are brought on line, they will substantially increase electrical generating capacity in the United States. The resurgence of interest in the construction of new nuclear power plants has also resulted in applications to construct and operate facilities for the manufacturing of nuclear fuel (e.g. uranium milling and enrichment). The NRC will perform safety, security, and environmental reviews of enrichment facility applications, a uranium deconversion facility application, and applications for uranium recovery facilities.

The NRC ensures safety and security by licensing and overseeing nuclear waste and spent fuel storage facilities, certifying storage and transportation containers, and responding to events, as well as through decontamination and decommissioning activities. Additionally, security plans, emergency preparedness, and security testing are a major part of the licensing, oversight, and other regulatory activities that provide high assurance of physical security for nuclear facilities and materials. The NRC further enhances its regulatory program through coordination and cooperation with other Federal agencies, States and international organizations and governments.

The NRC's FY 2013 Congressional Budget Justification provides the necessary resources for the Nuclear Reactor Safety and Nuclear Materials and Waste Safety Programs to carry out the agency's mission and achieve the stated goals and desired outcomes for the American public. The NRC's proposed FY 2013 budget is $1,053.2 million, including 3,951 full-time equivalents (FTE), which represents an increase of $15.1 million, including a decrease of 25 FTE, when compared with the FY 2012 enacted budget.

The Nuclear Reactor Safety Program increases by $9.7 million, including a decrease of 25 FTE; the Nuclear Materials and Waste Safety Program increases by $5.2 million, including a decrease of 0.3 FTE, when the FY 2013 request is compared with the FY 2012 enacted budget. Collectively, the Nuclear Reactor Safety and Nuclear Materials and Waste Safety Programs have an overall funding increase of $14.9 million, including a decrease of 26 FTE, when compared to the FY 2012 enacted budget.

The Office of the Inspector General's component of the FY 2013 proposed budget is $11.0 million and includes resources to carry out its mission to independently and objectively conduct audits and investigations to ensure the efficiency and integrity of NRC programs and operations and to promote cost-effective management.

Pursuant to the provisions of the Omnibus Budget Reconciliation Act of 1990, as amended, the NRC's FY 2013 budget provides for 90 percent fee recovery, less the amounts appropriated for (1) Waste Incidental to Reprocessing Activities under Section 3116 of the Ronald W. Reagan National Defense Authorization Act for Fiscal Year 2005 and (2) generic homeland security activities.

Budget Authority and Full-Time Equivalents (Dollars in Millions)						
	FY 2012 Enacted		FY 2013 Request		Delta FY 2013–FY 2012	
Major Programs	$M	FTE	$M	FTE	$M	FTE
Operating Reactors	534.7	2100.4	545.1	2074.7	10.4	(25.8)
New Reactors	265.4	924.6	264.8	925.0	(0.6)	0.4
Nuclear Reactor Safety Subtotal	$800.1	3,025.0	$809.9	2,999.6	$9.7	(25.4)
Fuel Facilities	56.1	228.4	56.1	226.8	0.1	(1.6)
Nuclear Materials Users	93.0	344.7	93.3	341.5	0.3	(3.1)
Spent Fuel Storage and Transportation	40.8	155.1	44.6	162.4	3.8	7.3
Decommissioning and Low-Level Waste	37.3	142.1	38.3	139.3	1.1	(2.8)
High-Level Waste Repository	0.0	0.0	0.0	0.0	0.0	0.0
Nuclear Materials and Waste Safety Subtotal	$227.1	870.4	$232.3	870.1	$5.2	(0.3)
Inspector General	10.9	58.0	11.0	58.0	0.2	0.0
Subtotal	$10.9	58.0	$11.0	58.0	$0.2	0.0
Reimbursable FTE		23.2		23.7		0.5
Total	$1,038.1	3,976.6	$1,053.2	3,951.4	$ 15.1	(25.2)

Numbers may not add due to rounding.

EXECUTIVE SUMMARY

Total NRC Budget Authority by Appropriation (Dollars in Millions)			
	FY 2012 Enacted	FY 2013 Request	Delta FY 2013–FY 2012
NRC Appropriations			
Salaries and Expenses (S&E)			
Budget Authority	1,027.2	1,042.2	15.0
Offsetting Fees	899.7	914.8	15.1
Net Appropriated S&E	127.5	127.4	(0.1)
Office of the Inspector General			
Budget Authority	10.9	11.0	0.2
Offsetting Fees	9.8	9.9	0.1
Net Appropriated OIG	1.1	1.1	0.0
Total NRC			
Budget Authority	1,038.1	1,053.2	15.1
Offsetting Fees	909.5	924.8	15.3
Total Net Appropriated	**$128.6**	**$128.5**	**($0.1)**

Numbers may not add due to rounding.

Accordingly, $924.8 million of the FY 2013 budget will be recovered from fees assessed to NRC licensees. This will result in a net appropriation of $128.5 million, which is a decrease of $0.1 million in net appropriations when compared with the FY 2012 enacted budget. In accordance with the requirements defined in Section 51.2 of the Office of Management and Budget (OMB) Circular A-11, Requirements for Program Justification, the NRC is providing the full cost of its programs.

Consistent with OMB guidance, the NRC's FY 2013 budget request includes a 0.5 percent pay raise for January 2013. The FY 2013 budget contains FTE savings in office support functional areas of administrative services, human resources, information management, information technology, and financial management (including contract management). The NRC plans to compensate for the FTE reductions by implementing cost-conscious business solutions to eliminate duplicative processes in agency support functions.

The Nuclear Reactor Safety Program encompasses NRC efforts to license, regulate, and oversee civilian nuclear power, research, and test reactors in a manner that adequately protects public health and safety and the environment. This program also provides high assurance of the physical security of facilities and protection against radiological sabotage. This program contributes to the NRC's Safety and Security goals through the activities of the Operating Reactors and New Reactors Business Lines that regulate existing and new nuclear reactors to ensure their safe operation and physical security.

Overall resources requested in the FY 2013 budget for the Nuclear Reactor Safety Program are $809.9 million, including 3,000 FTE. This funding level represents an overall funding increase of $9.7 million, including a decrease of 25 FTE, when compared with the FY 2012 enacted budget.

An explanation of the changes between the FY 2013 budget and FY 2012 enacted budget levels is provided in the program chapters of this budget for each business line.

Operating Reactors

The Operating Reactors Business Line supports the licensing, oversight, rulemaking, international activities, research, and event response associated with the safe and secure operation of 104 civilian nuclear power reactors and 31 research and test reactors (RTRs). The FY 2013 budget request for Operating Reactors is $545.1 million, including 2,075 FTE. This represents an overall funding increase of $10.4 million, including a decrease of 26 FTE, when compared with the FY 2012 enacted budget. The major activities that the requested resources will support include the following:

> Conduct technical review for 950 licensing actions, including the review of approximately 11 power uprates and approximately 25 ongoing National Fire Protection Association (NFPA) 805 reviews for the approximately 45 reactors that will be in transition to a risk-informed, performance-based set of requirements.

> Continue review of eight license renewal applications and three new applications, as well as provide support for one expected Federal court appeal of a license renewal decision.

> Conduct 10 high-priority rulemaking activities, support approximately 15 petitions for rulemaking (PRMs), including issuance of five closure packages.

Business Line	Nuclear Reactor Safety (Dollars in Millions)					
	FY 2012 Enacted		FY 2013 Request		Delta FY 2013–FY 2012	
	$M	FTE	$M	FTE	$M	FTE
Operating Reactors	534.7	2,100.4	545.1	2,074.7	10.4	(25.8)
New Reactors	265.4	924.6	264.8	925.0	(0.6)	0.4
Total	$800.1	3,025.0	$809.9	2,999.6	$9.7	(25.4)

Numbers may not add due to rounding.

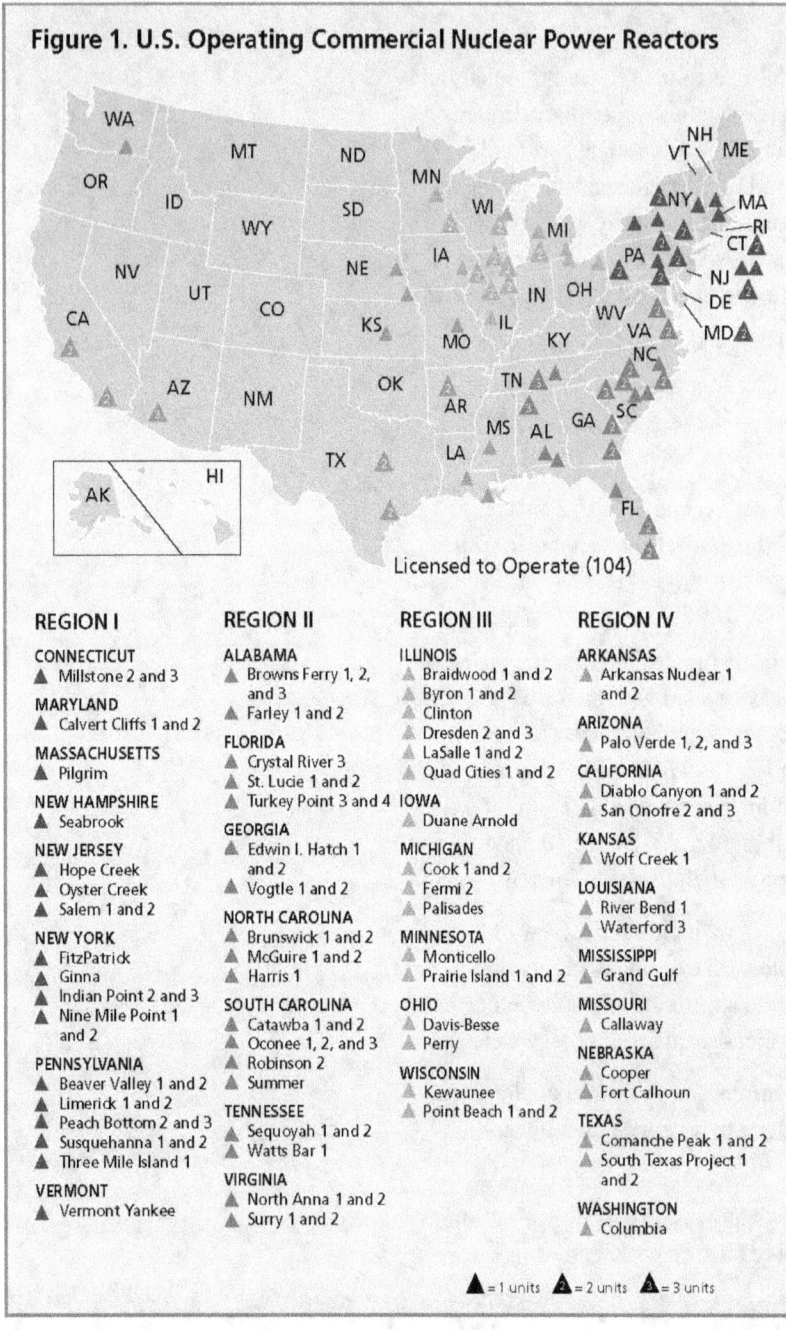

Figure 1. U.S. Operating Commercial Nuclear Power Reactors

Licensed to Operate (104)

REGION I

CONNECTICUT
▲ Millstone 2 and 3

MARYLAND
▲ Calvert Cliffs 1 and 2

MASSACHUSETTS
▲ Pilgrim

NEW HAMPSHIRE
▲ Seabrook

NEW JERSEY
▲ Hope Creek
▲ Oyster Creek
▲ Salem 1 and 2

NEW YORK
▲ FitzPatrick
▲ Ginna
▲ Indian Point 2 and 3
▲ Nine Mile Point 1 and 2

PENNSYLVANIA
▲ Beaver Valley 1 and 2
▲ Limerick 1 and 2
▲ Peach Bottom 2 and 3
▲ Susquehanna 1 and 2
▲ Three Mile Island 1

VERMONT
▲ Vermont Yankee

REGION II

ALABAMA
▲ Browns Ferry 1, 2, and 3
▲ Farley 1 and 2

FLORIDA
▲ Crystal River 3
▲ St. Lucie 1 and 2
▲ Turkey Point 3 and 4

GEORGIA
▲ Edwin I. Hatch 1 and 2
▲ Vogtle 1 and 2

NORTH CAROLINA
▲ Brunswick 1 and 2
▲ McGuire 1 and 2
▲ Harris 1

SOUTH CAROLINA
▲ Catawba 1 and 2
▲ Oconee 1, 2, and 3
▲ Robinson 2
▲ Summer

TENNESSEE
▲ Sequoyah 1 and 2
▲ Watts Bar 1

VIRGINIA
▲ North Anna 1 and 2
▲ Surry 1 and 2

REGION III

ILLINOIS
▲ Braidwood 1 and 2
▲ Byron 1 and 2
▲ Clinton
▲ Dresden 2 and 3
▲ LaSalle 1 and 2
▲ Quad Cities 1 and 2

IOWA
▲ Duane Arnold

MICHIGAN
▲ Cook 1 and 2
▲ Fermi 2
▲ Palisades

MINNESOTA
▲ Monticello
▲ Prairie Island 1 and 2

OHIO
▲ Davis-Besse
▲ Perry

WISCONSIN
▲ Kewaunee
▲ Point Beach 1 and 2

REGION IV

ARKANSAS
▲ Arkansas Nuclear 1 and 2

ARIZONA
▲ Palo Verde 1, 2, and 3

CALIFORNIA
▲ Diablo Canyon 1 and 2
▲ San Onofre 2 and 3

KANSAS
▲ Wolf Creek 1

LOUISIANA
▲ River Bend 1
▲ Waterford 3

MISSISSIPPI
▲ Grand Gulf

MISSOURI
▲ Callaway

NEBRASKA
▲ Cooper
▲ Fort Calhoun

TEXAS
▲ Comanche Peak 1 and 2
▲ South Texas Project 1 and 2

WASHINGTON
▲ Columbia

▲ = 1 units   ▲ = 2 units   ▲ = 3 units

> Conduct critical RTR project management functions pertaining to license renewal applications.

> Continue inspection activities for the 104 operating nuclear power plants, including the component design-basis inspections, fire protection inspections, and generic issues inspections (approximately 100 per year).

> Continue resident inspector pipeline initiative to maintain an experienced and stable onsite inspection presence of qualified resident inspectors at the 104 nuclear power plants.

> Conduct domestic and international security reviews and support for screening of approximately 3,000 national and international operational events with detailed evaluation of approximately 200 of those events.

> Evaluate licensee emergency preparedness during biennial exercises that include assessment of offsite response activities by the Federal Emergency Management Agency (FEMA).

> Conduct activities expected to review safety in response to the Fukushima lessons learned and long-term review.

New Reactors

The New Reactors Business Line supports the licensing, oversight, rulemaking, international activities, and research associated with the safe and secure development of new power reactors from design, site approval, and construction to operational status. The FY 2013 budget request for New Reactors is $264.8 million, including 925 FTE. This represents an overall funding decrease of $0.6 million, including an increase of 0.4 FTE, when compared with the FY 2012 enacted budget. The major activities that the requested resources will support include the following:

> Perform licensing and hearing support for review of 10 combined operating licenses (COLs).

> Continue review of two new DCs; continue review of one DC renewal; and start the review of three new DCs.

> Review two early site permit (ESP) applications and begin review of two new applications expected in FY 2013.

> Support licensing amendment requests for post-COL activities. The NRC expects that at least 10 percent of amendments will be for significant design changes associated with resolving first-of-a-kind construction issues.

> Provide oversight of six reactors expected to be under construction.

> Continue inspection of construction and preoperational testing activities for Watts Bar 2 to support operation in FY 2013.

> Perform work on three high-priority rulemakings and one medium-priority rulemaking.

> Perform work associated with advanced reactor technologies and preapplication reviews for small modular reactors (SMR).

NUCLEAR MATERIALS AND WASTE SAFETY

The Nuclear Materials and Waste Safety Program encompasses the NRC's effort to license, regulate, and oversee nuclear materials and waste in a manner that adequately protects public health and safety and the environment. This program provides high assurance of physical security of the most risk-significant materials and waste and protection against radiological sabotage, theft, or diversion of nuclear materials. Through this program, the NRC regulates uranium processing and fuel facilities; research and pilot facilities; nuclear materials users (medical, industrial, research, academic); spent fuel storage; spent fuel storage casks and transportation packaging; decontamination and decommissioning of facilities; and low-level and high-level radioactive waste. The program contributes to the NRC's Safety and Security goals through the activities of the Fuel Facilities, Nuclear Materials Users, Spent Fuel Storage and Transportation, and Decommissioning and Low-Level Waste Business Lines regulating byproduct, source, and SNM.

Nuclear Materials and Waste Safety (Dollars in Millions)						
Business Line	FY 2012 Enacted		FY 2013 Request		Delta FY 2013–FY 2012	
	$M	FTE	$M	FTE	$M	FTE
Fuel Facilities	56.1	228.4	56.1	226.8	0.1	(1.6)
Nuclear Materials Users	93.0	344.7	93.3	341.5	0.3	(3.1)
Spent Fuel Storage and Transportation	40.8	155.1	44.6	162.4	3.8	7.3
Decommissioning and Low-Level Waste	37.3	142.1	38.3	139.3	1.1	(2.8)
High-Level Waste Repository	0.0	0.0	0.0	0.0	0.0	0.0
Total	$227.1	870.4	$232.3	870.1	$5.2	(0.3)

Numbers may not add due to rounding.

Overall resources requested in the FY 2013 budget for the Nuclear Materials and Waste Safety Program are $232.3 million, including 870 FTE. This funding level represents an overall funding increase of $5.2 million, including a decrease of 0.3 FTE, when compared with the FY 2012 enacted budget.

Fuel Facilities

The Fuel Facilities Business Line supports licensing, oversight, rulemaking, international activities, research, generic homeland security, and event response associated with the safe and secure operation of various operating and new fuel facilities such as conversion, enrichment, and fuel fabrication facilities, and nuclear fuel research and pilot facilities. The FY 2013 budget request for Fuel Facilities is $56.1 million, including 227 FTE. This represents an overall funding increase of $0.1 million, including a decrease of 2 FTE, when compared with the FY 2012 enacted budget. The major activities that the requested resources will support include the following:

> Conduct licensing and oversight activities associated with fuel facilities and licensees with greater than critical mass quantities of SNM.

> Operate and maintain the Nuclear Material Management and Safeguards System database and the Nuclear Materials Information Program.

> Perform emergency preparedness, security, and licensee performance reviews.

> Conduct licensing, certification, inspection, oversight, environmental review, research, adjudicatory, enforcement, allegation, and other regulatory activities associated with new and operating fuel facilities, including uranium conversion and enrichment and fuel fabrication.

> Provide significant oversight of construction activities at the following facilities: Mixed Oxide (MOX) Fuel Fabrication Facility, Louisiana Energy Services (LES), U.S. Enrichment Corporation/American Centrifuge Project (USEC/ACP), AREVA, General Electric-Hitachi, and International Isotopes.

> Improve the fuel cycle oversight process and infrastructure to make them more effective, efficient, risk-informed, performance-based, transparent, and predictable.

Nuclear Materials Users

The Nuclear Materials Users Business Line supports the licensing, oversight, rulemaking, international activities, research, event response, and Agreement State activities associated with the safe and secure possession, processing, handling, and use of nuclear materials for the many and diverse uses of these materials. The FY 2013 budget request for Nuclear Materials Users is $93.3 million, including 342 FTE. This represents an overall funding increase of $0.3 million, including a decrease of 3 FTE, when compared with the FY 2012 enacted budget. The major activities that the requested resources will support include the following:

> Complete 2,500 materials licensing actions and 1,000 routine health and safety inspections.

> Conduct event evaluation, research, incident response, allegation, investigations, enforcement, and rulemaking activities to maintain the regulatory safety and

security infrastructure needed to process and handle nuclear materials.

❯ Perform materials activities related to State, Tribal, and Federal programs, including oversight, technical assistance, regulatory development, and cooperative efforts.

❯ Operate the National Source Tracking System (NSTS), a secure, Web-based, nationalized central registry designed to enhance the accountability for radioactive sources.

❯ Provide maintenance and operation support for the Integrated Source Management Portfolio (ISMP),

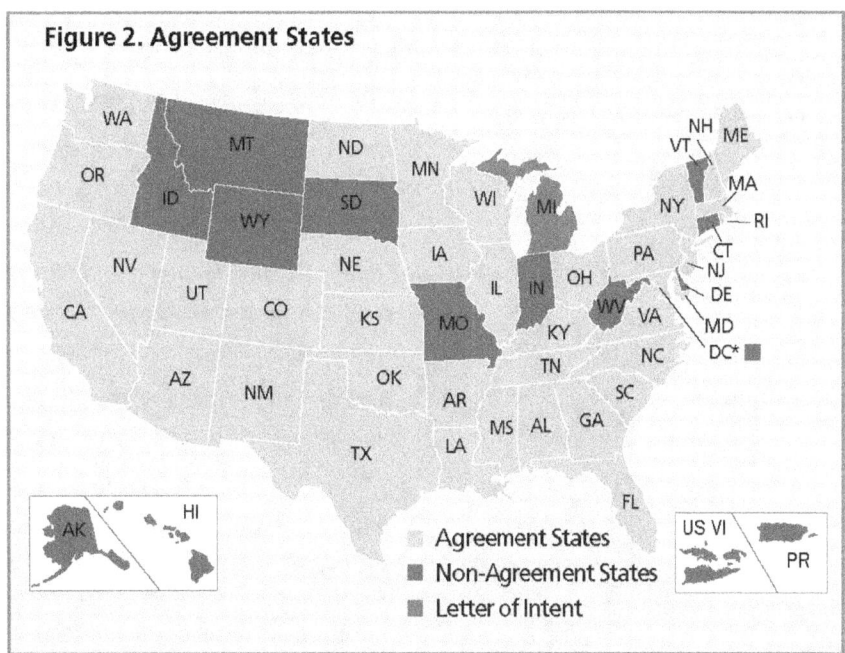

Figure 2. Agreement States

Agreement States
Non-Agreement States
Letter of Intent

which includes three core systems (NSTS, Web Based Licensing, and License Verification System) to track sources and other radioactive materials under one management mechanism.

❯ Conduct Integrated Materials Performance Evaluation Program reviews (10–12), continue outreach to potential new Agreement States and process new agreements (1), and process Agreement State incidents or events (50).

❯ Complete reviews and make decisions on import/export authorizations of nuclear components and radiological materials.

❯ Conduct investigations of wrongdoing, materials-related enforcement actions, oversight of the Alternative Dispute Resolution (ADR) and Allegation Programs, and external safety culture program activities.

Spent Fuel Storage and Transportation

The Spent Fuel Storage and Transportation Business Line supports the licensing, oversight, rulemaking, international activities, research, and event response associated with the safe and secure storage and transportation of spent nuclear fuel (SNF). The FY 2013 budget request for Spent Fuel Storage and Transportation is $44.6 million, including 162 FTE. This represents an overall funding increase of $3.8 million, including 7 FTE, when compared with the FY 2012 enacted budget. The major activities that the requested resources will support include the following:

❯ Review license requests for site-specific independent spent fuel storage installations (ISFSIs), dual-purpose (storage and transport) casks, transportation security plans, and route approvals to support safe and secure domestic and international transportation of radioactive materials, regulatory requirements for full-core offload capability at operating reactor sites, and transfer of spent fuel to ISFSIs to support reactor decommissioning.

> Identify and implement regulatory improvements to the proficiency and effectiveness of the licensing, inspection, and enforcement programs associated with the storage and transportation of SNF.

> Inspect storage cask and transportation cask vendors, fabricators, and designers and ISFSI pad construction, dry-run operations, initial loading operations and routine operations to ensure safety.

> Resolve technical issues associated with allowance of burnup credit for transportation and storage casks and the transportation and storage of high-burnup fuels (greater than 45 gigawatt-days/metric tons of uranium).

> Develop and execute a plan to develop a long-term waste confidence (WC) rule for the handling and extended storage of SNF for more than 60 years after a reactor's licensed life.

> Identify and resolve regulatory issues associated with extended storage and transportation of SNF and initial development of a licensing regulatory framework to accommodate alternative geologic disposal or other disposition options in response to changes in the national program for high-level waste (HLW) management.

> Conduct rulemaking efforts on ISFSIs that will provide consistent regulation for the various types and locations.

> Coordinate with domestic and international partners on the safety and security of storage and transport.

Decommissioning and Low-Level Waste

The Decommissioning and Low-Level Waste Business Line supports the licensing, oversight, rulemaking, international activities, and research associated with the safe and secure operation of uranium recovery facilities, removal of a nuclear facility from service and reduction of residual radioactivity to a level that permits release of the property and termination of the NRC license, and the disposition of low-level radioactive waste from all civilian sources. The FY 2013 budget request for Decommissioning and Low-Level Waste is $38.3 million, including 139 FTE. This represents an overall funding increase of $1.1 million, including a decrease of 3 FTE, when compared with the FY 2012 enacted budget. The major activities that the requested resources will support include the following:

> Conduct project management and technical reviews for decommissioning activities for 13 power and early demonstration reactors, 9 RTRs, 22 decommissioning complex materials facilities, and 38 decommissioning uranium recovery facilities.

> Work on 8 environmental and 11 safety reviews (hearings included) of applications, as well as licensing activities associated with 14 operating uranium recovery facilities.

> Provide assistance to the International Atomic Energy Agency (IAEA), the Nuclear Energy Agency, the IAEA's Waste Safety Standards Committee, the Joint Convention on the Safety of Spent Fuel Management and on the Safety of

Radioactive Waste Management, and many other working groups and committees for the preparation and updating of safety guides and standards.

❯ Provide oversight of certain U.S. Department of Energy (DOE) waste determination activities and plans consistent with the NRC's responsibilities in the Ronald W. Reagan National Defense Authorization Act for Fiscal Year 2005 to conduct Waste Incidental to Reprocessing activities.

High-Level Waste Repository

No resources have been budgeted for this business line since FY 2011.

OFFICE OF THE INSPECTOR GENERAL

In accordance with the Inspector General Act of 1978, as amended, the OIG's mission is to (1) independently and objectively conduct and supervise audits and investigations related to NRC programs and operations, (2) prevent and detect fraud, waste, and abuse, and (3) promote economy, efficiency, and effectiveness in NRC programs and operations. The OIG carries out its mission through its Audits and Investigations Programs. The NRC OIG Strategic Plan will be updated but currently features the following three goals that guide the activities of its Audits and Investigations Programs and generally align with the agency's mission:

OIG Strategic Goals

❯ Strengthen the NRC's efforts to protect public health and safety and the environment.

❯ Enhance the NRC's efforts to increase security in response to an evolving threat environment.

❯ Increase the economy, efficiency, and effectiveness with which the NRC manages and exercises stewardship over its resources.

OIG's proposed FY 2013 budget is $11.0 million, including 58 FTE staff. In accordance with OMB requirements, OIG is providing the full cost of its programs, in that the budget identifies OIG's management and operational support costs and distributes these costs proportionately to the Audits and Investigations Programs.

Overview of the OIG Budget (Dollars in Millions)						
Summary	FY 2012 Enacted		FY 2013 Request		Delta FY 2013–FY 2012	
	$M	FTE	$M	FTE	$M	FTE
Program Support	1.406		1.392		0.116	
Program Salaries & Benefits	9.454	58.0	9.628	58.0	0.044	0.0
Total	$10.860	58.0	$11.020	58.0	$0.160	0.0

Numbers may not add due to rounding.

Audits Program

With these resources, the Audits Program will conduct approximately 22 audits and evaluations. For FY 2013, the Audits Program will focus on agency programs involving the major management challenges and risk areas facing the NRC, to include those agency programs concerning new reactors and spent fuel storage and transportation. Areas for OIG audit emphasis in FY 2013 include the following:

> ❯ NRC oversight of the existing fleet of commercial nuclear reactors and the construction of new reactor plants.

> ❯ NRC oversight of the security and safety of nuclear materials.

> ❯ NRC actions to adequately secure sensitive information, technology, and databases.

> ❯ NRC regulatory activities involving the interim storage of high-level waste and spent fuel both at and away from the reactor facilities.

OIG will conduct other performance audits to review the NRC's administrative and program operations and evaluate the effectiveness and efficiency with which management responsibilities are carried out and whether the programs achieve intended results. Financial audits will also be conducted to evaluate the agency's financial programs. OIG will also conduct forensic audits as an outgrowth of its continuous monitoring program.

Investigations Program

The Investigations Program will initiate approximately 60 investigations and Event Inquiries. Areas for OIG investigative emphasis in FY 2013 include the following:

> ❯ Monitor NRC activities and gather stakeholder information to identify potential gaps in the NRC Reactor Oversight Process.

> ❯ Review NRC and licensee reports and engage interested stakeholders to identify issues of concern in NRC oversight of nuclear material held by its licensees.

> ❯ Examine efforts made by the NRC to address stakeholders' concerns regarding low-level and high-level waste storage issues.

> ❯ Address the NRC's efforts to oversee licensee responsibilities for effectively securing licensed facilities and nuclear materials.

> ❯ Conduct investigations into internal and external cyber breaches of the NRC's information technology infrastructure.

> ❯ Examine allegations of misuse of the NRC's corporate management resources to include personnel, procurement, financial, and information technology.

Proactive investigations are also conducted when indications are raised concerning potentially systematic violations such as theft of Government property or contract fraud. In addition, OIG periodically conducts Event Inquiries to identify staff actions that may have contributed to the occurrence of an event.

PROPOSED FY 2013
APPROPRIATIONS
LEGISLATION

APPROPRIATIONS LEGISLATION

The NRC's proposed appropriations legislation for FY 2013 is as follows:

SALARIES AND EXPENSES

For necessary expenses of the Commission in carrying out the purposes of the Energy Reorganization Act of 1974, as amended, and the Atomic Energy Act of 1954, as amended, including official representation expenses (not to exceed $25,000), $1,042,200,000, to remain available until expended: Provided, That revenues from licensing fees, inspection services, and other services and collections estimated at $914,832,000 in FY 2013 shall be retained and used for necessary salaries and expenses in this account, notwithstanding 31 U.S.C. 3302, and shall remain available until expended: Provided further, That the sum herein appropriated shall be reduced by the amount of revenues received during FY 2013 so as to result in a final FY 2013 appropriation estimated at not more than $127,368,000.

OFFICE OF THE INSPECTOR GENERAL

For necessary expenses of the Office of the Inspector General in carrying out the provisions of the Inspector General Act of 1978, as amended, $11,020,000, to remain available until September 30, 2014: Provided, That revenues from licensing fees, inspection services, and other services and collections estimated at $9,918,000, in FY 2013 shall be retained and be available until September 30, 2014, for necessary salaries and expenses in this account, notwithstanding 31 U.S.C. 3302: Provided further, That the sum herein appropriated shall be reduced by the amount of revenues received during FY 2013 so as to result in a final FY 2013 appropriation estimated at not more than $1,102,000.

ANALYSIS OF PROPOSED FY 2013 APPROPRIATIONS LEGISLATION

The analysis of the NRC's proposed appropriations legislation for FY 2013 is as follows:

Salaries and Expenses

1. For Necessary Expenses Of The Commission In Carrying Out The Purposes Of The Energy Reorganization Act Of 1974, As Amended, And The Atomic Energy Act Of 1954, As Amended:

42 U.S.C. 5841 et seq.

The NRC was established by the Energy Reorganization Act of 1974, as amended (42 U.S.C. 5801 et seq.). This act abolished the Atomic Energy Commission (AEC) and transferred to the NRC all of the AEC's licensing and related regulatory functions.

These functions included those of the Atomic Safety and Licensing Board Panel and the Advisory Committee on Reactor Safeguards; responsibilities for licensing and regulating nuclear facilities and materials; and conducting research for the purpose of confirmatory assessment related to licensing, regulation, and other activities, including research related to nuclear materials safety and regulation under the provisions of the Atomic Energy Act of 1954, as amended (42 U.S.C. 2011 et seq.).

2. Including Official Representation Expenses:

47 Comp. Gen. 657, 43 Comp. Gen. 305

This language is required because of the established rule restricting an agency from charging appropriations with the cost of official representation unless the appropriations involved are specifically available for such purpose. Congress has appropriated funds for official representation expenses to the NRC and its predecessor, the AEC, each year since FY 1950.

3. To Remain Available Until Expended:

31 U.S.C. 1301 provides that no regular, annual appropriation shall be construed to be permanent or available continuously unless the appropriation expressly provides that it is available after the fiscal year covered by the law in which it appears.

4. Revenues From Licensing Fees, Inspection Services, And Other Services And Collections Shall Be Retained And Used For Necessary Salaries And Expenses In This Account, Notwithstanding 31 U.S.C. 3302, And Shall Remain Available Until Expended:

Under Title V of the Independent Offices Appropriation Act of 1952, the NRC is authorized to collect license fees. Pursuant to 31 U.S.C. 9701, any person who receives a service or thing of value from the Commission shall pay fees to cover the NRC's cost in providing such service or thing of value.

Pursuant to 42 U.S.C. 2214, the NRC is required to assess and collect annual charges from NRC licensees and certificate holders, with the exception of the holders of any license for a federally owned research reactor used primarily for educational training and academic research purposes. In accordance with amendments to 42 U.S.C. 2214, enacted in the Energy Policy Act of 2005, and this appropriations request, the aggregate annual amount of such charges shall approximate 90 percent of the Commission's budget authority, less amounts appropriated to the Commission to implement Section 3116 of the Ronald W. Reagan National Defense Authorization Act for Fiscal Year 2005 and amounts appropriated to the Commission for generic homeland security activities.

Section 3116 of the Ronald W. Reagan National Defense Authorization Act for Fiscal Year 2005, Public Law (P.L.) 108-375, assigns new responsibilities to NRC for waste determinations and monitoring of waste disposal actions for material stored at the U.S. Department of Energy (DOE) sites in South Carolina and Idaho. Section 3116(b)

(4) requires that, beginning with the FY 2006 budget, the Commission include in its budget justification materials submitted to Congress the amounts required, not offset by revenues, for performance of its responsibilities under Section 3116. The $1,411,000 requested to implement Section 3116 is excluded from NRC's fee recovery requirements.

Section 637 of the Energy Policy Act of 2005, P.L. 109-58, modifies NRC's user fee legislation in 42 U.S.C. 2214 to exclude from license fee recovery the amounts appropriated to the Commission for homeland security activities, except for reimbursable costs of fingerprinting and background checks and the costs of conducting security inspections. The $24,309,000 requested for generic homeland security activities is excluded from NRC's fee recovery requirements.

The aggregate amount of license fees and annual charges to be collected for FY 2013 approximates 90 percent of the Commission's budget authority, less amounts requested to implement Section 3116 of the Ronald W. Reagan National Defense Authorization Act for Fiscal Year 2005 and amounts requested for generic homeland security activities pursuant to Section 637 of P.L. 109-58.

31 U.S.C. 3302 requires the NRC to deposit all revenues collected to miscellaneous receipts of the Treasury unless specifically authorized by law to retain and use such revenues.

5. The Sum Herein Appropriated Shall Be Reduced By The Amount Of Revenues Received:

Pursuant to 42 U.S.C. 2214, the NRC is required to assess and collect annual charges from NRC licensees and certificate holders, with the exception of the holders of any license for a federally owned research reactor used primarily for educational training and academic research purposes. In accordance with amendments to 42 U.S.C. 2214, enacted in the Energy Policy Act of 2005, and this appropriations request, the aggregate annual amount of such charges shall approximate 90 percent of the Commission's budget authority, less amounts appropriated to the Commission to implement Section 3116 of the Ronald W. Reagan National Defense Authorization Act for Fiscal Year 2005 and amounts appropriated to the Commission for generic homeland security activities.

Office of the Inspector General

6. For Necessary Expenses Of The Office Of The Inspector General In Carrying Out The Provisions Of The Inspector General Act Of 1978, As Amended:

P. L. 95-452, 5 U.S.C. app., as amended by P. L. 100-504

P. L. 100-504 amended P. L. 95-452 to establish an Office of the Inspector General in the NRC effective April 17, 1989, and to require the establishment of a separate appropriation account to fund the Office of the Inspector General.

Safety—develop, maintain, and implement licensing and regulatory programs for reactors.

Security—review security plans and changes for consistency with security requirements.

7. To Remain Available Until September 30, 2014:

31 U.S.C. 1301 provides that no regular, annual appropriation shall be construed to be permanent or available continuously unless the appropriation expressly provides that it is available after the fiscal year covered by the law in which it appears.

8. Revenues From Licensing Fees, Inspection Services, And Other Services And Collections Shall Be Retained And Be Available Until September 30, 2014, For Necessary Salaries And Expenses In This Account, Notwithstanding 31 U.S.C. 3302:

Under Title V of the Independent Offices Appropriation Act of 1952, the NRC is authorized to collect license fees. Pursuant to 31 U.S.C. 9701, any person who receives a service or thing of value from the Commission shall pay fees to cover the NRC's cost in providing such service or thing of value.

Pursuant to 42 U.S.C. 2214, the NRC is required to assess and collect annual charges from NRC licensees and certificate holders, with the exception of the holders of any license for a federally owned research reactor used primarily for educational training and academic research purposes. In accordance with amendments to 42 U.S.C. 2214, enacted in the Energy Policy Act of 2005, and this appropriations request, the aggregate annual amount of such charges approximate 90 percent of the Commission's budget authority, less amounts appropriated to the Commission to implement Section 3116 of the Ronald W. Reagan National Defense Authorization Act for Fiscal Year 2005 and amounts appropriated to the Commission for generic homeland security activities.

31 U.S.C. 3302 requires the NRC to deposit all revenues collected to miscellaneous receipts of the Treasury unless specifically authorized by law to retain and use such revenue.

9. The Sum Herein Appropriated Shall Be Reduced By The Amount Of Revenues Received:

Pursuant to 42 U.S.C. 2214, the NRC is required to assess and collect annual charges from NRC licensees and certificate holders, with the exception of the holders of any license for a federally owned research reactor used primarily for educational training and academic research purposes. In accordance with amendments to 42 U.S.C. 2214, enacted in the Energy Policy Act of 2005, and this appropriations request, the aggregate annual amount of such charges approximate 90 percent of the Commission's budget authority, less amounts appropriated to the Commission to implement Section 3116 of the Ronald W. Reagan National Defense Authorization Act for Fiscal Year 2005 and amounts appropriated to the Commission for generic homeland security activities.

NUCLEAR
REACTOR
SAFETY

NUCLEAR REACTOR SAFETY

The Nuclear Reactor Safety Program encompasses U.S. Nuclear Regulatory Commission (NRC) efforts to ensure that civilian nuclear power and research and test reactors (RTRs) are licensed and operated in a manner that adequately protects public health and safety, protects the environment, and ensures assurance of the physical security of reactor facilities. This program contributes to the NRC's Safety and Security goals through activities of the Operating Reactors and New Reactors Business Lines that license and regulate existing and new nuclear reactors to ensure their safe operation and physical security. The Atomic Energy Act of 1954, as amended (AEA), and the Energy Reorganization Act of 1974, as amended, are the foundations for the NRC regulation of the Nation's civilian nuclear power industry.

Nuclear security is a high priority for the NRC. Throughout its history, effective regulation and strong partnerships with a variety of Federal, State, and local authorities have ensured security at civilian nuclear reactors across the country, especially power reactors. NRC recognizes the need for continuous improvement to ensure the safety and security of nuclear power plants. In recent years, the NRC has undertaken comprehensive enhancements to bolster the security of our Nation's nuclear facilities and radioactive materials.

At the time this budget was submitted, the Commission was considering the staff's proposed prioritization of the Fukushima Near-Term Task Force recommendations and regulatory actions to be taken in response to the events at Fukushima Daiichi. The NRC will ensure that regulatory changes necessary to maintain continued safety of the domestic nuclear energy will be accommodated and executed.

Safety—ensure adequate protection of public health and safety and the environment.

Security—ensure adequate protection in the secure use and management of radioactive materials.

Business Line	Nuclear Reactor Safety (Dollars in Millions)					
	FY 2012 Enacted		FY 2013 Request		Delta FY 2013–FY 2012	
	$M	FTE	$M	FTE	$M	FTE
Operating Reactors	534.7	2,100.4	545.1	2,074.7	10.4	(25.8)
New Reactors	265.4	924.6	264.8	925.0	(0.6)	0.4
Total	$800.1	3,025.0	$809.9	2,999.6	$9.7	(25.4)

Numbers may not add due to rounding.

PROGRAM RESOURCE SUMMARY

The FY 2013 proposed budget request for the Nuclear Reactor Safety Program is $809.9 million, which includes $349.4 million in contract support and travel and $460.5 million in salaries and benefits to support 2,999.6 full-time equivalents (FTE). This amount funds activities in the Operating Reactors and New Reactors Business Lines. When compared to the FY 2012 enacted budget, this request represents an increase of $9.7 million, including a reduction of 25.4 FTE due to fewer overhead FTE being allocated to the Reactor Safety program. The increase primarily supports regulatory activities associated with locating, licensing, and overseeing new and operating nuclear power plants and implementing lessons-learned recommendations from the near-term task force that studied the Fukushima Daiichi accident.

OPERATING REACTORS

Operating Reactors by Product Line (Dollars in Millions)						
Product Line	FY 2012 Enacted		FY 2013 Request		Delta FY 2013–FY 2012	
	$M	FTE	$M	FTE	$M	FTE
Licensing	89.5	477.3	86.7	451.9	(2.8)	(25.4)
Oversight	157.3	888.6	155.9	875.4	(1.4)	(13.2)
Rulemaking	13.3	60.9	13.7	62.8	0.4	1.9
Research	66.1	171.0	74.5	175.8	8.3	4.9
International Activities	2.3	13.5	4.5	17.9	2.2	4.4
Generic Homeland Security	6.5	25.1	4.8	22.9	(1.7)	(2.2)
Event Response	14.3	55.8	14.8	54.8	0.5	(0.9)
Subtotal	$349.4	1,692.1	$354.8	1,661.5	$5.4	(30.5)
Corporate Support	185.4	408.3	190.3	413.1	4.9	4.8
Total	$534.7	2,100.4	$545.1	2,074.7	$10.4	(25.8)

Numbers may not add due to rounding.

The Operating Reactors Business Line encompasses the regulation of 104 operating civilian nuclear power reactors and 31 Research and Test Reactors (RTRs) in a manner that adequately protects the health and safety of the public, protects the environment, and ensures high assurance of physical security. Under the regulatory oversight of the NRC, the amount of safe electrical power generated from the 104 domestic nuclear power plants now contributes approximately 20 percent of the Nation's electrical production.

The NRC establishes regulatory requirements for the design, construction, operation, and security of nuclear power plants and RTRs in accordance with the provisions of the Atomic Energy Act of 1954, as amended. Through Operating Reactors Business Line activities, the NRC ensures the fundamental tenets of its Safety and Security goals in protecting both the public and workers from the radiation hazards of nuclear reactors. To ensure plants are operating safely within these requirements, the NRC licenses the plants to operate, licenses the personnel who operate the plants, and establishes technical specifications for the operation of each plant. The NRC also ensures nuclear safety through rulemaking and research efforts, enforcement, and international activities. The NRC oversees civilian nuclear reactors and verifies operator adherence to the NRC's rules and regulations.

The NRC has undertaken comprehensive reviews to bolster the security of our Nation's nuclear facilities. Nuclear power plants must be able to defend successfully against a set of hypothetical threats that the agency refers to as the design-basis threat (DBT).

These hypothetical threats challenge a plant's physical security, personnel security, and cyber security. The agency continuously evaluates this set of hypothetical threats against real-world intelligence to ensure that it remains current and prepared.

The budgetary resources will enable the NRC to continue licensing and regulatory activities to ensure the safe and secure operation of these civilian nuclear reactors. The

NRC has developed product lines for operating reactors that best support safety and security strategies that affect its strategic outcomes as they relate to existing civilian reactors. The resources requested support the Operating Reactors Business Line within the following seven product lines: Licensing, Oversight, Rulemaking, Research, International Activities, Generic Homeland Security (HLS), and Event Response. The outputs of the product lines under this business line contribute to the scoring of the NRC Safety and Security performance measures and their contribution to the achievement of its strategic outcomes.

Changes From FY 2012 Enacted Budget

Resources in this business line increased primarily to implement lessons-learned recommendations from the near-term task force that studied the Fukushima Daiichi accident. Licensing resources decreased because the NRC was in the process of identifying the FY 2013 workload levels related to the Fukushima near-term task force at the time this budget was submitted. The licensing decrease was partly offset by anticipated increases in National Fire Protection Association (NFPA) 805 reviews. Resources allocated to oversight decreased because of a decline in overhead staffing which were partly offset by increases for work related to Fukushima, cyber security, and regional baseline inspection activities associated with a planned additional operating plant (Watts Bar 2). Rulemaking increases to support work related to Fukushima were partly offset by decreases resulting from the completion of work; they also provide funding for other higher priority research projects. Research resources increased to support work related to Level 3 probabilistic risk analysis (PRA) to incorporate insights from advances in PRA technology and research to evaluate hazards from natural events, including earthquakes, floods, and tsunami. International activities resources increased to support work related to a shift from generic HLS caused by changes to the budget structure. The same changes caused resources in generic HLS to decrease.

Licensing

For FY 2013, the NRC requests $86.7 million, including 451.9 FTE, to provide for licensing activities. This represents a funding decrease of $2.8 million, including a decrease of 25.4 FTE, when compared with the FY 2012 enacted budget. Licensing resources decreased because the NRC was in the process of identifying the FY 2013 workload levels related to the Fukushima near-term task force at the time this budget was submitted. The licensing decrease was partly offset by increases to meet the anticipated greater number of NFPA 805 reviews.

The Licensing Product Line supports licensing activities, which are the methods the NRC employs to establish requirements to ensure operating nuclear power reactor licensees, RTRs, and medical isotope production facility requests for license renewals and other changes provide an adequate margin of safety and security consistent with the NRC's rules and regulations.

The NRC also licenses civilian nuclear power reactors and nonpower reactors to ensure that they are operated in a manner that adequately protects the health and safety of the public, protects the environment, and ensures physical security.

Strategic Goal Strategies Supported by Licensing

Safety—*develop, maintain, and implement licensing and regulatory programs for reactors.*

Security—*review security plans and changes for consistency with security requirements.*

In FY 2013, the NRC will continue licensing activities for 104 power reactors. The NRC anticipates that the licensing workload will require completing 950 licensing actions, including the review of approximately 11 power uprates and approximately 25 ongoing NFPA 805 reviews for the approximately 45 reactors that will be in transition to a risk-informed, performance-based set of requirements.

Reviews will continue for eight license renewal applications for operating reactors. The NRC expects to review three new applications (covering four sites) and support one expected license renewal decision from the Federal Court of Appeals. The resources will support the development, maintenance, and implementation of the license renewal infrastructure, process assessments, improvements, and activities related to developing infrastructure for potential applications for license renewals.

The NRC will continue licensing reviews, issue license amendments, and perform project management activities for the existing 31 licensed operating nonpower reactors and ensuring that operators are qualified and licensed to perform their duties. In addition, the NRC will review applications for medical isotope production facilities as well as review the U.S. Department of Energy (DOE) fuel performance report and address the amendment for conversion of nonpower reactors from high-enriched to low-enriched uranium fuel. The NRC will complete 600 other licensing tasks and related activities, including assistance to the regions, interactions with vendors and owners' groups, and 15 technical topical report reviews that resolve generic issues. In addition, the NRC expects to complete approximately 55 operator licensing examination sessions and 4 generic tests for reactor operators.

Resources also support licensing activities such as the review of licensing amendments associated with the security plan changes, cyber security, emergency preparedness reviews, and license renewal activities and associated adjudication, legal advice, and representation. The NRC will continue Federal interactions with codes and standards organizations, such as the American Society of Mechanical Engineers and Institute of Electrical and Electronics Engineers along with other Federal agencies, such as the Federal Energy Regulatory Commission, on topics relating to coating guidance, grid stability, and digital instrumentation and control (I&C).

Oversight

For FY 2013, the NRC requests $155.9 million, including 875.4 FTE, for oversight activities. This represents a funding decrease of $1.4 million, including a decrease of 13.2 FTE, when compared with the FY 2012 enacted budget. Decreases in overhead staffing are partly offset by increases to support cyber security and regional baseline inspection activities associated with a planned additional operating plant (Watts Bar 2).

The Oversight Product Line supports the activities and methods the NRC employs to oversee the safe and secure operation of existing nuclear reactors, better identify significant performance issues, and ensure that licensees take appropriate actions to maintain acceptable operating performance to adequately protect public health and safety and the environment.

The NRC performs continuous oversight of plants through its Reactor Oversight Process (ROP) to verify that the 104 currently licensed nuclear power reactors are operated safely and securely in accordance with the NRC's rules, regulations, and license requirements. The NRC has full authority to take action to protect public

---

Strategic Goal Strategies Supported By Oversight

Safety—*continue to oversee the safe operation of existing plants; oversee licensee safety performance through inspections, investigations, enforcement, and performance assessment activities.*

Security—*evaluate licensee security and emergency preparedness programs; use force-on-force (FOF) inspections to test security.*

health and safety and can demand immediate licensee action, up to and including a plant shutdown. The ROP uses NRC inspection findings and performance indicators that are reported quarterly by licensees to assess the safety performance of each plant within a regulatory framework of seven cornerstones of safety and security (i.e., 1) frequency of potential accident-initiating events; 2) availability, reliability, and capability of mitigating systems; 3) integrity of radiation barriers, such as fuel cladding, reactor coolant system, and containment boundaries; 4) emergency preparedness; 5) protection of the public from radiation releases; 6) occupational radiation safety; and 7) physical protection against the DBT for radiological sabotage). The ROP recognizes that not all issues are equally significant. The ROP has a structure in place that creates more NRC engagement and oversight for events that are more significant. Plants are expected to address issues through their corrective action programs for events that are less significant. In this way, the oversight workload directly supports the Safety and Security goals and related strategic measures and outcomes.

Generally, the NRC performs two types of inspections: baseline and plant-specific. The FY 2013 budget request includes resources for planned baseline and anticipated plant-specific inspections. Historically, the resources required for these inspections have been fairly constant. A portion of the baseline inspection program is conducted on a 3-year cycle, including approximately 22 fire protection and 22 component design-basis inspections per year. Baseline inspections focus on plant activities, especially those that are not adequately measured by performance indicators. Resources also support plant-specific inspections that typically include 20 reactive inspections, 75 inspections related to performance or specific changes (e.g., inspections done at independent spent fuel storage installations, digital control room inspections), and approximately 100 generic issue inspections that address areas of emerging concern (e.g., cyber security or areas where recurring problems have occurred). The NRC conducts performance-based evaluations of licensee security and emergency preparedness programs and assesses their effectiveness. Security resources support the NRC's security inspection and assessment program with a number of key elements. These include baseline, triannual FOF, and special inspections and the development of the annual report to Congress. Current plans are to begin full implementation of the cyber security inspections in FY 2013. There will be a 2-year increase in regional work for target set and protective strategy inspections as a result of the new rule. The NRC conducts and performs baseline and special inspections of emergency preparedness to ensure that plants satisfy the requirements for responding to emergencies.

Resources also support enforcement allegation activities and investigations of alleged wrongdoing. Enforcement is used to deter noncompliance with NRC requirements and to encourage prompt identification and correction of violations.

The ROP also includes the Industry Trends Program through which the NRC collects, analyzes, displays, and trends industrywide reactor performance data to determine whether the data show statistically significant adverse industry trends in reactor safety performance.

Resources also support legal review; communications to internal and external stakeholders; audits associated with the ROP; license renewal inspections; Alternative Dispute Resolution Program activities (including contract management); performance assessments; and the development of inspection, assessment, and enforcement guidance and outreach activities with State and local governments, Tribal organizations, and interstate organizations.

Resources will support event evaluation, generic communications, and the review of industry operating experience (screening of approximately 3,000 national and international operational events per year). Approximately 150 to 200 issues per year receive additional detailed evaluations. Resources support independent evaluation and trending of operational events and fund evaluations of human factor events.

Resources also will support the maintenance and operation of the Reactor Programs System (RPS), which is used to plan and schedule inspection activities and capture and report of inspection findings. RPS is critical to supporting the oversight and inspection of the 104 nuclear power reactors and 31 nonpower reactors. This is an agencywide tool that supports 47 uranium recovery sites and 9 major fuel cycle facilities. The resources will also support simulator hardware and software maintenance for reactor technology training and Web development associated with reactor oversight.

Rulemaking

For FY 2013, the NRC requests $13.7 million, including 62.8 FTE, for rulemaking activities. This represents a funding increase of $0.4 million, including 1.9 FTE, when compared with the FY 2012 enacted budget. Rulemaking increases to support work related to Fukushima were partly offset by decreases that resulted from the completion of work; these increases also provide funding for other higher priority research projects.

The Rulemaking Product Line includes the development and update of rules, regulatory guidance, and standard review plans that promote licensee compliance with underlying safety principles and security requirements.

The regulatory framework guides the safety and security activities of the agency and its licensees. The NRC's rules and regulations contribute to the Safety and Security goals and related strategic measures and outcomes because they form the foundation for the safety and security activities of the agency. NRC regulations are contained in Title 10 of the Code of Federal Regulations (10 CFR), "Energy."

The FY 2013 workload includes 10 high-priority rulemaking activities. Resources provide support for work on approximately 15 petitions for rulemaking (PRMs), assume receipt of 6 PRMs each year, and support issuance of 5 closure packages. Resources will also support legal advice for high-priority rulemakings, five petitions, and regulatory basis development for potential proposed rulemakings.

Resources for rulemaking support the development and completion of the technical assessment and regulatory-basis development efforts that are needed to prepare and promulgate new or amended regulations for ongoing, new, and amended rules; develop supplemental regulatory guides or other guidance documents directly related to revised and new rules; and complete the Commission-directed Regulatory Guide Update Program. Resources also allow the NRC to continue maintaining rulemaking guidance documents based on lessons learned and process improvements/ enhancements, including work on regulatory guides. Support for other rulemaking activities includes updating and implementing guidance documents (e.g., NUREGs). Specifically, resources support rulemaking activities related to performance-based

STRATEGIC GOAL STRATEGIES
SUPPORTED BY RULEMAKING

Safety—*use sound science and state-of-the-art methods to establish, where appropriate, risk-informed and performance-based regulations.*

Security—*use a framework of rules and regulations to guide the security activities of the agency.*

acceptance criteria for the emergency core cladding system, fitness-for-duty (FFD) requirements, periodic 10 CFR 50.55a rulemakings, and integrity rules for reactor pressure vessels. In addition, resources support updates to regulatory analysis guidance in NUREG/BR-0058, Revision 4, "Regulatory Analysis Guidelines of the U.S. Nuclear Regulatory Commission," and in NUREG/BR-0184, "Regulatory Analysis Technical Evaluation Handbook."

Research

For FY 2013, the NRC requests $74.5 million, including 175.8 FTE, for research activities. This represents a funding increase of $8.3 million, including 4.9 FTE, when compared with the FY 2012 enacted budget. Research increases to support work related to Level 3 PRAs to incorporate insights from advances in PRA technology and research to evaluate the hazards from natural disasters, including seismic, flooding, and tsunami events.

The mission of the NRC's research program is to evaluate and resolve safety issues for nuclear power plants and other facilities and materials that the agency regulates. This includes evaluating of existing and potential safety issues; supplying independent expertise, information, and technical judgments to support timely and realistic regulatory decisions; reducing uncertainties in risk assessments; and developing technical regulations and standards. Research programs cover all technical areas of the NRC's regulations.

In FY 2013, research work will be performed in several technical areas to ensure the continued safety and security of operating reactors. These areas include fire safety, digital systems, materials degradation, risk assessment, and evaluation of hazards from natural events. The following describes the work planned.

Fire safety research will support the transition to a risk-informed, performance-based set of requirements in response to NFPA Standard 805 and the current licensing basis for plants. This work includes cable fire testing, spurious circuit actuation testing, fire-risk-assessment training, and fire modeling.

The NRC Digital System Research Plan includes the review of current and future applications of digital I&C, a failure mode and reliability assessment of software and digital systems, an aging assessment of components and equipment, and a review of the security aspects of digital systems. Additional support includes electrical research in the areas of equipment qualification for life beyond 60 years, aging assessment of electrical insulation materials, battery performance, impact of smart grids on nuclear power plants, and assessment of failure of onsite power sources.

Research will continue to further understand and manage potential degradation associated with reactor pressure boundary components, vessel internals, containment liners, and neutron-absorbing materials used in spent fuel pools. This research includes assessing the effectiveness and reliability of various inservice inspection techniques, performing residual stress and nondestructive examination studies on retired components, evaluating the behavior of various components under severe accident conditions, developing a probabilistic code for assessing piping integrity, and studying the embrittlement of reactor vessel pressure boundary materials. Research is also being performed in the area of material engineering to evaluate plant life extension beyond 60 years.

STRATEGIC GOAL STRATEGIES SUPPORTED BY RESEARCH

Safety—improve the NRC's regulatory programs and apply safety-focused research to anticipate and resolve safety issues.

Security—use research to inform the security activities of the agency.

STRATEGIC GOAL STRATEGIES SUPPORTED BY INTERNATIONAL ACTIVITIES

Safety—*use domestic and international operating experience to inform decision-making.*

Security—*work with international counterparts to exchange information.*

Research efforts include the development of plant-specific standardized plant analysis risk models and maintenance of the Systems Analysis Programs for Hands-on Integrated Reliability Evaluations software used for PRA to support the ROP. Resources also support the development of improved methods and tools for risk-informing regulatory programs, including the development of new PRA methods, models, and tools and the development of a site Level 3 PRA to incorporate insights from advances in PRA technology.

Research efforts will also include the evaluation of hazards from natural disasters, including seismic hazards, flooding, and tsunami events. These activities are conducted in cooperation with other Federal agencies (e.g., the U.S. Geological Survey, the National Oceanographic and Atmospheric Administration, the U.S. Army Corps of Engineers, and the U.S. Department of the Interior's Bureau of Reclamation), State agencies, academic institutions, and industry. The results of this research are used to inform licensing decisions and update risk assessments.

International Activities

For FY 2013, the NRC requests $4.5 million, including 17.9 FTE, for international activities. This represents a funding increase of $2.2 million, including 4.4 FTE, when compared with the FY 2012 enacted budget. International activities increase to support work related to a shift from generic HLS that resulted from changes to the budget structure.

The International Activities Product Line supports the NRC's mission of protecting public health and safety through international exchanges, which assist with decisionmaking, awareness of and responses to emerging technical issues, and best practices in realizing the Safety and Security goals and related strategic measures and outcomes. Additionally, the NRC participates in the development and evaluation of international standards to ensure that they are soundly based and to determine whether substantial safety improvement can be identified and implemented domestically. The NRC also must perform certain legislatively mandated international duties. These include licensing the import and export of nuclear materials and equipment and participating in activities supporting U.S. compliance with international treaties and agreement obligations. The NRC has bilateral programs to provide assistance or cooperation with 36 countries and Taiwan. In addition, the NRC actively cooperates with multinational organizations, such as the International Atomic Energy Agency (IAEA) and the Nuclear Energy Agency, part of the Organisation for Economic Co-operation and Development.

The International Activities Product Line workload includes periodic exchanges of information important to the safe operation of nuclear power plants, visits to construction and operating domestic nuclear power plants, assistance to foreign regulatory bodies through the NRC Foreign Assignee Program, and the review and decisions on applications for the export and import of nuclear equipment. The NRC assists the IAEA and individual countries through its bilateral agreements and participates in multilateral activities with other nations, such as the Convention on Nuclear Safety, the Joint Convention on the Safety of Spent Fuel Management and the Safety of Radioactive Waste Management, and IAEA's Integrated Regulatory Review Service and International Physical Protection Advisory Service missions.

The NRC supports activities associated with safety, security, and conversion of nonpower reactors and participates in international cooperative research programs that provide access to operating experience from foreign reactors to augment NRC programs in areas such as plant aging and materials degradation, fire risk, and pressurized thermal shock. Analysis of this experience contributes to the NRC's knowledge base, improves assessments of plant risk, and assists with the development of risk-informed approaches to regulation.

The NRC works with its international counterparts to exchange information, expertise, and operating experiences; participate in ongoing research to recognize and respond to emerging technical issues; and promote best safety and security practices. This international cooperation better informs NRC decisions and promotes nuclear safety and security worldwide.

Generic Homeland Security

For FY 2013, the NRC requests $4.8 million, including 22.9 FTE, for generic HLS activities. This represents a funding decrease of $1.7 million, including a decrease of 2.2 FTE, when compared with the FY 2012 enacted budget. Generic HLS decreases because of a shift to international activities that resulted from changes to the budget structure.

The Generic HLS Product Line supports security activities related to intergovernmental coordination and communication on intelligence, threat demographic data, and information security activities that are not related to information technology (IT). It also includes coordination and exchange of information among local, State, and Federal agencies on security-related matters, as well as security-related international activities.

In FY 2013, the Generic HLS Product Line workload includes the entire scope of threat assessment activities (intelligence information assessment, internal and external communications, and information assessment team activities), intergovernmental coordination on national HLS priorities, integrated response planning and coordination, emerging technology analysis and evaluation, and international security-related activities (IAEA and multilateral and bilateral cooperation). The workload also includes developing and enhancing the ability to make risk-informed analyses of accident progression and radiological releases to the environment in response to accidents and malevolent attacks.

Event Response

For FY 2013, the NRC requests $14.8 million, including 54.8 FTE, for event response activities. This represents a funding increase of $0.5 million, including a decrease of 0.9 FTE, when compared with the FY 2012 enacted budget— which does not represent a significant change in workload.

The Event Response Product Line supports the NRC's incident response and emergency preparedness activities to ensure that the agency can respond effectively to events at its licensees' sites and take adequate protective measures to mitigate plant damage and minimize possible radiation exposure to members of the public. Emergency preparedness ensures that nuclear power plant operators can protect public health and safety in the event of an emergency.

STRATEGIC GOAL STRATEGIES SUPPORTED BY GENERIC HOMELAND SECURITY

Safety—effectively respond to events at NRC-licensed facilities and other events of national interest, including maintaining and enhancing the NRC's critical incident response and communication capabilities.

Security—support Federal response plans that employ an approach to the security of nuclear facilities and radioactive material that integrates the efforts of licensees and Federal, State, local, and Tribal authorities.

STRATEGIC GOAL STRATEGIES SUPPORTED BY EVENT RESPONSE

Safety—effectively respond to events at NRC-licensed facilities and other events of national interest, including maintaining and enhancing the NRC's critical incident response and communication capabilities.

Security—support Federal response plans that employ an approach to the security of nuclear facilities and radioactive material that integrates the efforts of licensees and Federal, State, local, and Tribal authorities.

The NRC participates in emergency preparedness exercises, some of which include security and terrorism scenarios. As part of these exercises, the NRC works with licensees, Federal agencies, State and local officials, and first responders to form a coordinated system of emergency preparedness and response. This system includes public information, preparations for evacuation, instructions for sheltering, and other actions to protect residents.

Sharing information quickly among the NRC, other Federal agencies, and the nuclear industry is critical to preventing a terrorist attack. The NRC supports several important Federal antiterrorism centers for integrated assessments of security-related information. The NRC Headquarters Operations Center (HOC) is staffed around the clock to disseminate information and coordinate responses. To ensure the timely distribution of threat information, the NRC continuously reviews intelligence and assesses suspicious activity. As described in the National Response Framework, the NRC is the coordinating agency for events occurring at NRC-licensed facilities and those involving radioactive materials licensed either by the NRC or by an Agreement State.

In FY 2013, the workload includes drill and exercise preparations; event readiness activities; incident response communications; security coordination; and strategies for integrated response, emergency preparedness-related interfaces, secure communications and information management, and materials event evaluation and response. Resources also support the replenishment of potassium iodide tablet supplies that will expire in FY 2012 for States with a population within the 16.1-kilometer (10-mile) emergency planning zone of operating nuclear reactors. Resources support the Emergency Response Data System and the HOC Information Management System, which form the primary infrastructure to support the NRC's 24/7 capability to respond to radiological, nuclear materials, and national security events.

Funding also provides for the emergency telecommunications system, responder satellite phones, and the e-Library. Event response resources include secure communications and information activities for the continuity of operations and continuity of government and the Defense Red Switch Network.

Significant Accomplishments in FY 2011

The NRC responded to the nuclear emergency at Japan's Fukushima Daiichi nuclear facility and coordinated its actions with other Federal agencies as part of the U.S. Government's response. NRC emergency responders staffed the HOC for more than three months and closely monitored the status of the Fukushima Daiichi reactors and spent fuel pools. Such an extreme set of circumstances led to a fast-paced response effort with a large degree of uncertainty about plant conditions. However, consistent with the agency's domestic response mission, the NRC did everything that could be done to ensure that U.S. citizens living in Japan and elsewhere were safe. In responding to this unique challenge, the NRC identified a number of good practices and lessons-learned items that the NRC is using to improve its response program. The event in Japan also demonstrated the ability of the NRC to conduct continuous and effective response operations. Following the Fukushima Daiichi accident, the NRC established a task force to conduct a systematic and methodical review of the NRC's processes and regulations to determine whether the agency should make additional improvements to its regulatory system and to make recommendations for the Commission's policy direction.

In FY 2011 the Nation's nuclear power plants were operated within the NRC safety and security requirements. The performance measures for the Safety goal confirmed that nuclear power plants were operating safely. In addition, the safety indicators for nuclear plants showed no adverse trends.

The NRC engaged in multiple emergency exercises with its licensees and Federal partners. NRC emergency responders participated in 20 exercises with licensee sites across the country, 4 of which involved the NRC Headquarters Response Team. These exercises focused on the implementation of onsite and offsite radiological emergency plans by the licensee, as well as State and local responders. The NRC also used exercises to train its response organization and practice coordination activities with Federal partners, including the U.S. Department of Homeland Security.

The NRC participated in one hostile-action-based (HAB) emergency preparedness drill, conducted voluntarily at the River Bend Station, and coordinated with the Federal Emergency Management Agency (FEMA) to observe numerous other HAB drills to gain a better understanding of the unique challenges hostile action events pose and to identify significant good practices and lessons learned.

The NRC successfully maintained vigilant oversight of security in the nuclear industry and implemented the agency's security procedures within its baseline security inspection program. This inspection effort resides within the Security Cornerstone of the agency's ROP. The Security Cornerstone focuses on the following five key licensee performance attributes: access authorization, access control, physical protection systems, material control and accounting, and response to contingency events. Through the results obtained from all oversight activities, including baseline security inspections and performance indicators, the NRC determines whether licensees comply with requirements and can provide high assurance of adequate protection against the DBT for radiological sabotage.

The NRC research program addressed key areas that support the agency's safety mission. Some of the important issues include verification and validation of fire safety models; material degradation of reactor system and pressure boundary components, especially as it relates to license renewal periods; evaluation of digital systems to analyze failure modes; research on hazards from natural disasters, including seismic hazards issues, flooding, and tsunami events; development of advanced tools for PRA activities that support risk-informed regulatory decisionmaking; severe reactor accident consequence analyses; and reactor thermal-hydraulic analyses.

The NRC renewed 12 operating licenses. This major accomplishment is the culmination of extensive staff reviews, audits, and inspections for each license renewal application. The NRC has renewed a total of 71 operating licenses since it established the license renewal program in FY 2000.

NUCLEAR REACTOR SAFETY

Operating Reactors Output Measures

Licensing

Completion of License Renewal Application Reviews						
	FY 2008	FY 2009	FY 2010	FY 2011	FY 2012	FY 2013
Target	Complete major milestones for 3 applications.	Complete major milestones for 4 applications.	Complete major milestones for 3 applications.	Complete major milestones for 3 applications.	Make final decision on license renewal for 1 reactor unit.	Make final decision on license renewal for 2 reactor units.
Actual	Renewed 2 licenses. Completed SER and SEIS for 2 plants.	Renewed 4 licenses.	Renewed 5 licenses. Completed SER for 3 applications and SEIS for 2 applications.	Renewed 8 licenses.		

Licensing Actions Completed per Year						
	FY 2008	FY 2009	FY 2010	FY 2011	FY 2012	FY 2013
Target	Complete 1,465 licensing actions.	Complete 1,150 licensing actions.	Complete 950 licensing actions.	Complete 950 licensing actions.*	Complete 950 licensing actions.*	Complete 950 licensing actions.*
Actual	1,054 completed	1,002 completed	988 completed	849 completed**		

*As limited by the number of licensing action requests submitted/accepted the previous FY.

Age of the Other Licensing Task Inventory*						
	FY 2008	FY 2009	FY 2010	FY 2011	FY 2012	FY 2013
Target	90% ≤ 1 yr. 100% ≤ 2 yrs.	90% ≤ 1 yr. 100% ≤ 2 yrs.	90% ≤ 1 yr. 100% ≤ 2 yrs.	90% ≤ 1 yr. 100% ≤ 2 yrs.	90% ≤ 1 yr. 100% ≤ 2 yrs.	90% ≤ 1 yr. 100% ≤ 2 yrs.
Actual	96.6% ≤ 1 yr. 100% ≤ 2 yrs.	90% ≤ 1 yr. 100% ≤ 2 yrs..	94% ≤ 1 yr. 100% ≤ 2 yrs.	94.2% < 1 yr. 99.6% < 2yrs.		

*As limited by the number of licensing action requests submitted/accepted the previous FY.

Age of Licensing Action Inventory*						
	FY 2008	FY 2009	FY 2010	FY 2011	FY 2012	FY 2013
Target	90% ≤ 1 yr. 100% ≤ 2 yrs.	93% ≤ 1 yr. 100% ≤ 2 yr	90%** ≤ 1 yr. 100% ≤ 2 yrs.	95% ≤ 1 yr. 100% ≤ 2 yrs	95% ≤ 1 yr. 100% ≤ 2 yrs.	95% ≤ 1 yr. 100% ≤ 2 yrs.
Actual	94.6% ≤ 1 yr 100% ≤ 2 yrs.	94% ≤ 1 yr. 100% ≤ 2 yrs.	93% ≤ 1 yr. 100% ≤ 2 yr.	90.3% < 1 yr. 99.9% < 2 yrs.**		

* Excludes license renewal and improved standard technical specifications (iSTS) conversions. Also excludes license amendment requests that are unusually complex.
** Though targets not met, the trends during the third and fourth quarters of FY 2011 were upward. Exceeding the 2-year target was the result of recordkeeping error.

Other Licensing Tasks Completed per Year						
	FY 2008	FY 2009	FY 2010	FY 2011	FY 2012	FY 2013
Target	Complete 600 other licensing tasks.	Complete 600 other licensing tasks.	Complete 600 other licensing tasks.	Complete 600 other licensing tasks.	Complete 600 other licensing tasks.	Complete 600 other licensing tasks.*
Actual	678 other licensing tasks completed.	541 other licensing tasks completed.	625 other licensing tasks completed.	465 other licensing tasks completed.**		

*As limited by the number of other licensing task requests submitted/accepted the previous FY.

**Other licensing task inventory reduction efforts in FY 2010 and operational events during FY 2011 resulted in not meeting the target.

Number Of Operator Licensing Examinations Administered					
	FY 2008	FY 2009	FY 2010	FY 2011	FY 2012	FY 2013
Target	Meet licensee demand estimated at 50 initial operator licensing examination sessions and 4 generic fundamentals examination sessions.	Meet licensee demand estimated at 55 initial operator licensing examination sessions and 4 generic fundamentals examination sessions.	Meet licensee demand estimated at 55 initial operator licensing examination sessions and 4 generic fundamentals examination sessions.	Meet licensee demand estimated at 55 initial operator licensing examination sessions and 4 generic fundamentals examination sessions.	Meet licensee demand estimated at 55 initial operator licensing examination sessions and 4 generic fundamentals examination sessions.	Meet licensee demand estimated at 55 initial operator licensing examination sessions and 4 generic fundamentals examination sessions.
Actual	Met licensee demand estimated at 50 initial operator licensing examination sessions and 4 generic fundamentals examination sessions.	Met licensee demand estimated at 59 initial operator licensing examination sessions and 4 generic fundamentals examination sessions.	Met licensee demand estimated at 54 initial operator licensing examination sessions and 4 generic fundamentals examination sessions.	Met licensee demand estimated at 55 initial operating licensing examination sessions and 4 generic fundamentals examination sessions.		

Oversight

Number of Plants for Which the Baseline Inspection Program Was Completed During The Most Recently Ended Inspection Cycle*					
	FY 2008	FY 2009	FY 2010	FY 2011	FY 2012	FY 2013
Target	All required baseline inspection procedures are completed at 103 operating reactors.	All required baseline inspection procedures are completed at 104 operating reactors.	All required baseline inspection procedures are completed at 104 operating reactors.	All required baseline inspection procedures are completed at 104 operating reactors.	All required baseline inspection procedures are completed at 104 operating reactors.	All required baseline inspection procedures are completed at 104 operating reactors.
Actual	Completed all reactors.	Completed all reactors.	Completed all reactors.	Cannot be validated for the 2011 calendar year baseline cycle until mid-February 2012. Preliminary information indicates on track for successful completion.		

*The ROP inspection program is implemented on a calendar-year (CY) basis; therefore, the baseline inspection program was not fully implemented in CY 2007 for Browns Ferry 1, as it was restarted that year after an extended shutdown. The baseline inspection program metric includes 104 operating reactors, including Browns Ferry 1 starting in CY 2008.

Percentage of Final Significance Determination Process Determinations Made Within 90 Days for All Potentially Greater Than Green Findings					
	FY 2008	FY 2009	FY 2010	FY 2011	FY 2012	FY 2013
Target	90%	90%	90%	90%*	90%	90%
Actual	100%	100%	93%	100%		

* Target mistakenly reported to be 100% in 2011 Congressional Budget Justification.

Time to Complete Reviews of Technical Allegations*

	FY 2008	FY 2009	FY 2010	FY 2011	FY 2012	FY 2013
Target	80% ≤ 150 days 90% ≤ 180 days 100% ≤ 360 days	90% ≤ 150 days 95% ≤ 180 days 100% ≤ 360 days	90% ≤ 150 days 95% ≤ 180 days 100% ≤ 360 days	90% ≤ 150 days 95% ≤ 180 days 100% ≤ 360 days	90% ≤ 150 days 95% ≤ 180 days 100% ≤ 360 days	90% ≤ 150 days 95% ≤ 180 days 100% ≤ 360 days
Actual	93% ≤ 150 days 98% ≤ 180 days 99% ≤ 360 days*	93% ≤ 150 days 98% ≤ 180 days 99% ≤ 360 days*	95% ≤ 150 days 98% ≤ 180 days 100% ≤ 360 days	98% ≤ 150 days 99% ≤ 180 days 100% ≤ 360 days		

*A few allegations exceeded the target due to complicated technical review or extended review at another Federal agency.

Timeliness in Completing Enforcement Actions*

	FY 2008	FY 2009	FY 2010	FY 2011	FY 2012	FY 2013
Target	Investigation cases: 100% completed within 360 days of OE processing time. Noninvestigation cases: 100% completed within 180 days of OE processing time.	Investigation cases: 100% completed within 360 days of OE processing time. Noninvestigation cases: 100% completed within 180 days of OE processing time.	Investigation cases: 100% completed within 360 days of OE processing time. Noninvestigation cases: 100% completed within 180 days of OE processing time.	Investigation cases: 100% completed within 360 days of OE processing time. Noninvestigation cases: 100% completed within 180 days of OE processing time.	Investigation cases: 100% completed within 330 days of OE processing time. Noninvestigation cases: 100% within 160 days of OE processing time.	Investigation cases: 100% completed within 330 days of OE processing time. Noninvestigation cases: 100% within 160 days of OE processing time.
Actual	Investigation: One ≥ 360 days Noninvestigation: none ≥ 180 days	Investigation: None ≥ 360 days Noninvestigation: none ≥ 180 days	Investigation: None ≥ 360 days Noninvestigation: none ≥ 180 days	Investigation: None ≥ 360 days Noninvestigation: none ≥ 180 days		

A. Cases involving investigations normally involve wrongdoing, including discrimination, and by their nature are more resource intensive and less timely. Accordingly, the performance measure for cases involving investigations provides for more staff time.

B. Office of Enforcement (OE) processing time is defined as that time from the date the case is opened or the licensee is briefed on the concern (exit) to the issuance of an enforcement action or other appropriate disposition less: (1) any time the NRC could not act due to the case residing with U.S. Department of Labor, U.S. Department of Justice, or other government entity or where the licensee or anyone outside the enforcement process causes a lengthy deferment, and (2) any time the NRC could not act due to processing Freedom of Information Act (FOIA) requests.

Timeliness in Completing Investigations–Target 1

	FY 2008	FY 2009	FY 2010	FY 2011	FY 2012	FY 2013
Target	80% of investigations that developed sufficient information to reach a conclusion regarding wrongdoing will be completed in 10 months or less.	80% of investigations that developed sufficient information to reach a conclusion regarding wrongdoing will be completed in 10 months or less.	80% of investigations that developed sufficient information to reach a conclusion regarding wrongdoing will be completed in 10 months or less.	80% of investigations that developed sufficient information to reach a conclusion regarding wrongdoing will be completed in 10 months or less.	80% of investigations that developed sufficient information to reach a conclusion regarding wrongdoing will be completed in 10 months or less.	80% of investigations that developed sufficient information to reach a conclusion regarding wrongdoing will be completed in 9 months or less.
Actual	Completed 77 investigations in which 92.2% (67) developed sufficient information to reach a conclusion regarding wrongdoing were completed in 10 months or less.	Completed 106 investigations in which 98.1% (104) developed sufficient information to reach a conclusion regarding wrongdoing were completed in 10 months or less.	Completed 40 investigations in which 98% (39) developed sufficient information to reach a conclusion regarding wrongdoing were completed in 9 months or less.	Completed 93 investigations; 84% (78) developed sufficient information to reach a conclusion regarding wrongdoing were completed in 9 months or less		

Timeliness in Completing Investigations–Target 2					
	FY 2008	FY 2009	FY 2010	FY 2011	FY 2012	FY 2013
Target	Close 100% of OI investigations in time to initiate civil and/or criminal enforcement action.	Close 100% of OI investigations in time to initiate civil and/or criminal enforcement action.	Close 100% of OI investigations in time to initiate civil and/or criminal enforcement action.	Close 100% of OI investigations in time to initiate civil and/or criminal enforcement action.	Close 100% of OI investigations in time to initiate civil and/or criminal enforcement action.	Close 100% of OI investigations in time to initiate civil and/or criminal enforcement action.
Actual	Closed 100% of OI investigations in time to initiate civil and/or criminal enforcement action.	Closed 100% of OI investigations in time to initiate civil and/or criminal enforcement action.	Closed 100% of OI investigations in time to initiate civil and/or criminal enforcement action.	Closed 100% of OI investigations in time to initiate civil and/or criminal enforcement action.		

Research

Timeliness of Completing Actions on Critical Research Programs*					
	FY 2008	FY 2009	FY 2010	FY 2011	FY 2012	FY 2013
Target	90% of major milestones met on or before their due date.	90% of major milestones met on or before their due date.	90% of major milestones met on or before their due date.	90% of major milestones met on or before their due date.	90% of major milestones met on or before their due date.	90% of major milestones met on or before their due date.
Actual	100% across programs.	100% across programs.	100% across programs.	100% across programs.		

*Critical research programs typically respond to high-priority needs from the Commission and NRC's licensing organizations. Critical research programs will be the highest priority needs identified at the beginning of each FY.

Acceptable Technical Quality of Agency Research Technical Products*					
	FY 2008	FY 2009	FY 2010	FY 2011	FY 2012	FY 2013
Target	Combined score ≥ 3.0	Combined score ≥ 3.5	Combined score ≥ 3.5	Combined score ≥ 3.5	Combined score ≥ 3.5	Combined score ≥ 3.5
Actual	4	4	4.6	4.8		

*The NRC has developed a process to measure the quality of research products using surveys of end-users to determine the usability and value-added of the products. As appropriate, other mechanisms will be developed and added to this process to measure the quality of research products.

Event Response

Emergency Response Performance Index*					
	FY 2008	FY 2009	FY 2010	FY 2011	FY 2012	FY 2013
Target	100%	100%	100%	100%	100%	100%
Actual	100%	100%	100%	100%		

*This performance index provides a single overall performance measure of the agency's readiness to respond to a nuclear or terrorist emergency situation or other events of national interest. The index measures several activities within the Incident Response Program that are critical in supporting the agency's preparedness and response ability.

Efficiency

Transitioning from Hard-Copy Distribution of Outgoing Licensee Correspondence to Electronic Distribution					
	FY 2008	FY 2009	FY 2010	FY 2011	FY 2012	FY 2013
Target	New measure in FY 2011.			$80,000 reduction	Measure discontinued	
Actual						

Minimize Necessary Communication Systems Devices for Senior Manager Use					
	FY 2008	FY 2009	FY 2010	FY 2011	FY 2012	FY 2013
Target	New measure in FY 2012.				$410,000 reduction.	
Actual						

Revise Inspection Process*					
	FY 2008	FY 2009	FY 2010	FY 2011	FY 2012	FY 2013
Target	New measure in FY 2011.			$500,000 reduction	Measure discontinued**	Measure discontinued
Actual				Target met.		

*The staff reviewed inspection findings and the significance of the findings, the resources used, and the effectiveness of the procedure per Inspection Manual Chapter 307, "Reactor Oversight Process Self-Assessment Program." A biennial review of baseline procedure effectiveness is being used to realign inspection resources to ensure they are applied in the most effective way overall.
**A one-time reduction was made in 2011, and the budget will stay constant at the reduced 2011 level.

| Product Line | New Reactors by Product Line (Dollars in Millions) | | | | | |
| | FY 2012 Enacted | | FY 2013 Request | | Delta FY 2013–FY 2012 | |
	$M	FTE	$M	FTE	$M	FTE
Licensing	131.9	483.1	123.2	467.5	(8.7)	(15.6)
Oversight	35.7	197.1	40.2	215.3	4.6	18.2
Rulemaking	1.8	9.0	1.4	7.1	(0.5)	(1.9)
Research	9.6	37.0	10.6	34.8	1.0	(2.3)
International Activities	1.6	9.5	1.1	6.9	(0.4)	(2.6)
Generic Homeland Security	0.8	3.6	1.2	4.2	0.3	0.6
Subtotal	$181.3	739.4	$177.6	735.7	($3.7)	(3.7)
Corporate Support	84.1	185.2	87.2	189.3	3.1	4.0
Total	$265.4	924.6	$264.8	925.0	($0.6)	0.4

Numbers may not add due to rounding.

The work of the New Reactors Business Line responds to the industry's renewed interest in building new commercial nuclear power plants to meet the Nation's future electric power generation needs. All civilian nuclear power reactors must be licensed by the NRC and adhere to NRC regulations to operate in the United States. Renewed demand and national policy initiatives, such Department of Energy's (DOE's) Nuclear Power 2010 program and the Energy Policy Act of 2005, have stimulated a nuclear resurgence. The New Reactors Business Line is responsible for the regulatory activities associated with locating, licensing, and overseeing construction of new nuclear power reactors. The NRC reviews new nuclear power reactor design certification (DC), combined license (COL), and early site permit (ESP) applications consistent with 10 CFR Part 52, "Licenses, Certifications, and Approvals for Nuclear Power Plants," and industry's projected plans and schedules. The NRC also reviews new nuclear power reactor construction permit and operating license applications consistent

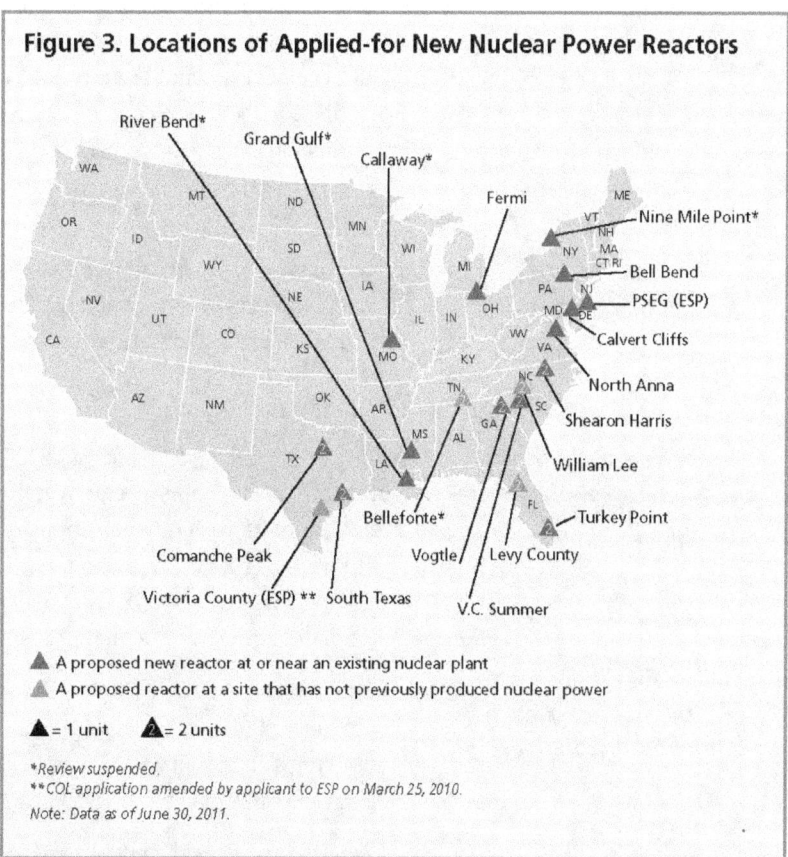

Figure 3. Locations of Applied-for New Nuclear Power Reactors

▲ A proposed new reactor at or near an existing nuclear plant
▲ A proposed reactor at a site that has not previously produced nuclear power

▲ = 1 unit   ▲ = 2 units

*Review suspended.
**COL application amended by applicant to ESP on March 25, 2010.
Note: Data as of June 30, 2011.

with 10 CFR Part 50, "Domestic Licensing of Production and Utilization Facilities." The new reactor activities ensure that the development of new civilian nuclear power reactor facilities is done in a manner that protects the health and safety of the public, protects the environment, and provides high assurance of security.

The NRC has streamlined the application process for new reactors under 10 CFR Part 52, including publishing a major revision in FY 2008. By issuing a COL, the NRC authorizes the licensee to construct and, with specified conditions, operate a nuclear power plant at a specific site. The application process prescribed under 10 CFR Part 50, which was implemented for all currently operating reactors, involves separate applications for the issuance of a construction permit and an operating license.

The NRC continues to interact with vendors and utilities regarding prospective new reactor applications and licensing activities.

The NRC has shifted its activities from developing the infrastructure to support the technical reviews of large, light-water reactors to performing the technical reviews and developing the infrastructure to support construction inspection and small modular reactors (SMRs). The NRC will continue the development and implementation of the construction inspection program, provide oversight of the construction activities at Watts Bar 2, and conduct vendor inspections. Oversight activities will increase to support industry construction schedules. These activities include supporting inspections of key international nuclear equipment and component suppliers and continuing license examiner training. In addition, the NRC will begin to review multiple SMR applications.

The NRC has organized new reactor activities into product lines that best support Safety and Security strategies and affect Strategic Outcomes as they relate to new civilian reactors. The resources requested support all direct aspects of new reactors within the following six product lines: Licensing, Oversight, Rulemaking, Research, International Activities, and Generic Homeland Security. The outputs of the product lines under this business line contribute to the scoring of the NRC Safety and Security Performance Measures and their contribution to the achievement of its Strategic Outcomes.

Changes From FY 2012 Enacted Budget

The decrease is the result of FY 2013 being the final year of buildout for a new Headquarters office building and a reduction in preapplication activities for advanced reactors, because the staff will be reviewing actual licensing applications in FY2013.

Licensing

For FY 2013, the NRC requests $123.2 million, including 467.5 FTE, for licensing activities. This represents an overall funding decrease of $8.7 million, including a decrease of 15.6 FTE, when compared with the FY 2012 enacted budget. The decrease is the result of FY 2013 being the final year of buildout for a new Headquarters office building and a reduction in preapplication activities for advanced reactors, because the staff will be reviewing actual licensing applications in FY2013.

The Licensing Product Line supports the licensing process—the NRC's determination that applicants' plans for the development, construction, and operation of new nuclear power plants provide an adequate margin of safety and security to ensure protection of public health and safety and the environment, consistent with the NRC's rules and regulations.

Licensing includes the review and certification of new and advanced reactor designs and development of a regulatory framework, including the supporting technical basis to license advanced reactor designs.

Workload includes continuing to review COL and operating License applications (safety, environmental, and other program reviews), including meetings before the Advisory

Committee on Reactor Safeguards and hearing preparations before the Atomic Safety and Licensing Board Panel. A COL, issued by the NRC, authorizes the licensee to construct and, with specified conditions, operate a nuclear power plant at a specific site. As of December 2011, the NRC is currently actively reviewing 12 of the 18 COL applications it has received from the nuclear power industry. NRC expects to complete the licensing process for three applications in FY 2012 and to continue work on 10 COL applications during FY 2013. The FY 2013 budget request includes resources to review all applications.

Resources will fund environmental reviews; safety reviews, which include emergency preparedness technical reviews, security plan technical reviews, and security-related assessments; and financial analysis of COL applicants. Licensing also provides the resources to support licensing-related legal representation, independent advice, and adjudicatory reviews; IT for licensing activities; an operator licensing system; scheduler support; and the regulatory infrastructure for licensing activities.

The NRC issues a DC to certify a standard nuclear plant design that is independent of a specific site. This DC is valid for 15 years. Budgetary resources for licensing during FY 2013 will support the ongoing review of two DCs (U.S. EPR and U.S. Advanced Pressurized-Water Reactor (US-APWR)), continued review of one DC renewal (Advanced Boiling-Water Reactor (ABWR)), and review of three new DCs (Korea Electric Power Corporation, Westinghouse SMR, and NuScale).

Licensing resources support the review of two ESP applications received in FY 2010 and the initiation of a review of two new applications expected in FY 2013, as well as the expected reactivation of construction and licensing for Bellefonte 1.

Resources also support licensing amendments for post-COL activities. The NRC expects that at least 10 percent of amendments will be for important or significant design changes associated with resolving first-of-a-kind construction issues. Resources will also continue to support review and evidentiary hearing activities; licensing-related legal advice and representation, independent advice, and adjudicatory reviews; and the regulatory infrastructure for postlicensing.

Licensing resources support preapplication review for three SMR DCs: Babcock & Wilcox mPower, Westinghouse and NuScale. These resources also permit the NRC to maintain awareness of Next Generation Nuclear Plant activities and conduct related research.

Funding is included in the New Reactor Program to support the final buildout of a new Headquarters office building. Additionally, resources are included to support one-time costs for the purchase and installation of secure (classified) communications and IT connections and equipment required for the functionality of the NRC's new headquarters operation center (HOC) and Sensitive Compartmented Information Facilities.

The new reactors licensing support begins to shift from developing large, light-water reactor regulatory infrastructure necessary infrastructure to support advanced reactor licensing activities. These resources support incorporating interim staff guidance and lessons learned into regulatory guides and standard review plans (SRP); beginning the 3-year update of the SRP; developing and maintaining other staff guidance, and contract support for scheduling staff reviews. Resources continue to support the staff's effort to resolve identified policy and key technical issues facing SMRs. In addition, these resources support the implementation of issue resolutions by developing both new and revised rules and guidance documents. Resources also development and implementation of technical bases for anticipated SMR applications.

Oversight

For FY 2013, the NRC requests $40.2 million, including 215.3 FTE, for oversight activities. This represents a funding increase of $4.6 million, including 18.2 FTE, when compared with the FY 2012 enacted budget. This increase is due to the inspection of six reactors under construction and the increase in vendor inspections to 30. In addition, upon official notification of its intent to reactivate construction and completion of Bellefonte 1 theTennessee Valley Authority, the NRC will begin to review various programs related to assessing the current condition of the facility under the quality verification program and other activities required by the Deferred Plant Policy Statement.

The Oversight Product Line provides resources to support construction inspection activities. During FY 2013, the NRC will develop and implement construction inspection activities to support inspection of six reactors under construction (Vogtle Units 3 and 4, Summer Units 2 and 3, South Texas Project Unit 3, and Watts Bar Unit 2). Oversight includes resources needed for increased enforcement-related casework, construction and vendor allegations, and investigations of wrongdoing. The NRC will continue inspection of construction and preoperational testing activities for Watts Bar 2 to support operation in FY 2013. For Bellefonte 1, the NRC will continue its inspections under the Deferred Plant Policy Statement regarding maintenance, preservation, and documentation activities and the program to assess the condition of the facility. Budgetary resources support an increase for up to 30 vendor inspections in FY 2013 to ensure integrity of the supply chain, consistent with the expected increase in the number of suppliers and sites under active construction. Also, the NRC will support the continued implementation of a formal agencywide program to monitor and evaluate counterfeit, fraudulent, and suspect items, as developed in FY 2011.

Oversight seeks to verify that the new reactor construction process ensures the adequate protection of public health and safety, protects the environment, and provides high assurance of the security of facilities through the verification that plants are constructed to the requirements established during the licensing process.

Resources also support the development and implementation of a cyber security inspection program. Current plans are to conduct several pilot cyber security inspections and workshops in FY 2012. This will support final development of the training program for inspectors, the inspection procedure, and the enforcement policy for new reactor cyber security inspections.

In FY 2013, resources support training, development, and construction of new reactor simulators at the Technical Training Center, the training development of new licensing examiners, and support for the fitness-for-duty program (FFD), including the operation and maintenance of the electronic reporting systems for FFD performance reports.

Rulemaking

For FY 2013, the NRC requests $1.4 million, including 7.1 FTE, for rulemaking activities. This represents an overall funding decrease of 0.5 million, including a decrease of 1.9 FTE, when compared with the FY 2012 enacted budget, which does not represent a significant change in workload.

The Rulemaking Product Line supports activities to maintain the safety and security framework of rules, regulatory guidance, and Standard Review Plans. This framework promotes licensee compliance with underlying safety principles and security requirements. In FY 2013, resources support work on three high-priority rulemakings, of which two are directly related to DC activities and on the 10 CFR Part 21, rulemaking and associated guidance development to (in part) resolve commitments in response to Inspector General audits. These resources also support one medium-priority Commission-directed rulemaking related to amending Appendix I, to numerical guides for design objectives and limiting conditions for operation to meet the criterion as low as is reasonably achievable for radioactive material in light-water-cooled nuclear power reactor effluents, "to 10 CFR Part 50, and incorporate International Corporation on Radiological Protection recommendations

International Activities

For FY 2013, the NRC requests $1.1 million, including 6.9 FTE, to provide for international activities. This represents an overall funding decrease of $0.4 million, including a decrease of 2.6 FTE, when compared with the FY 2012 enacted budget. The decrease is a result of the reclassification of resources for international technical assistance activities from the Nuclear Reactors Safety Program to the Corporate Support Program.

The International Product Line supports the NRC's interface with international counterparts to exchange information, expertise, operating experience, and research results. These activities help the NRC recognize and respond to emerging technical issues and promote best safety and security practices. Resources support the continued participation in the Multinational Design Evaluation Program that will continue international exchanges of licensing and construction inspection activities to potentially increase safety at U.S. sites.

Research

For FY 2013, the NRC requests $10.6 million, including 34.8 FTE, for research activities. This represents an overall funding increase of $1.0 million, including a decrease of 2.3 FTE, when compared with the FY 2012 enacted budget, which does not represent a significant change in workload.

The mission of the NRC's research program is to evaluate and resolve safety issues for nuclear power plants and other facilities and materials that the agency regulates. This includes evaluating existing and potential safety issues; supplying independent expertise, information, and technical judgments to support timely and realistic regulatory decisions; reducing uncertainties in risk assessments; and developing technical regulations and standards.

New reactors research funding supports resolving technical issues in DC reviews; developing of regulatory guidance for new reactor licensing; advancing the NRC's knowledge of, and infrastructure for, earthquake engineering; and developing of new reactor plant models. Research resources also support the advanced reactors program, including the development of expertise, tools, and data in areas such as thermal-hydraulics, severe accidents and probabilistic risk assessment, human factors, materials performance, and seismic/structural analysis. Advanced reactor program research will support the review of SMRs.

STRATEGIC GOAL STRATEGIES SUPPORTED BY INTERNATIONAL ACTIVITIES

Safety—*use domestic and international operating experience to inform decision making.*

Security—*work with international counterparts to exchange information.*

STRATEGIC GOAL STRATEGIES SUPPORTED BY RESEARCH

Safety—*improve the NRC's regulatory programs and apply safety-focused research to anticipate and resolve safety issues.*

Security—*use research to inform the security activities of the agency.*

STRATEGIC GOAL STRATEGIES
SUPPORTED BY GENERIC
HOMELAND SECURITY

Safety—effectively respond
to events at NRC-licensed
facilities and other events
of national interest,
including maintaining and
enhancing the NRC's critical
incident response and
communication capabilities.

Security—support Federal
response plans that employ
an approach to the security
of nuclear facilities and
radioactive material that
integrates the efforts of
licensees and Federal, State,
local, and Tribal authorities.

Generic Homeland Security

For FY 2013, the NRC requests $1.2 million, including 4.2 FTE, for generic homeland security activities. This represents a funding increase of $0.3 million, including 0.6 FTE, when compared with the FY 2012 enacted budget, which does not represent a significant change in workload.

Resources support new reactor security guidance development, infrastructure, and program management in support of licensing activities, development of standard review plan, and infrastructure for the consistent review of security-related areas of licensing applications.

Significant Accomplishments in FY 2011

The NRC continued the technical and safety reviews of 12 COL amendments, 3 DC applications, and 2 DC amendments and issued final safety evaluation reports for 2 COLs. The NRC prepared and issued the proposed rulemakings for the AP1000 DC amendment, the ABWR DC amendment, and the General Electric Economic Simplified Boiling-Water Reactor (ESBWR) DC and is preparing the final rulemaking packages for these rulemakings. The environmental reviews of four COL applications were completed through the issuance of the final environmental impact statements (EIS) for the following sites: South Texas Project, V. C. Summer, Calvert Cliffs, and Comanche Peak.

In addition, the staff completed the final supplemental environmental impact statement for the Vogtle COL application. The NRC began its safety and environmental reviews of two ESP applications that were submitted in FY 2010 and initiated prelicensing activities for a new ESP application expected in FY 2012.

The NRC began to address significant policy issues related to the licensing of advanced reactors and continued to make significant progress on refining the processes for overseeing construction activities.

New Reactors Output Measures

Licensing

Review Early Site Permit Applications on the Schedules Negotiated with the Applicants.

	FY 2008	FY 2009	FY 2010	FY 2011	FY 2012	FY 2013
Target	Complete 1 ESP review (North Anna). Continue review of 1 existing ESP application (Vogtle).	Complete 1 ESP review (Vogtle).	No ESPs planned for FY 2010.	No ESPs planned for FY 2011.	Review Victoria and PSEG applications.*	Continue Victoria and PSEG reviews. Begin review of Blue Castle and Callaway applications.
Actual	Issued ESP on North Anna, Vogtle ESP review on schedule.	Issued Vogtle ESP review on schedule.	Completed milestones for 2 ESP reviews (Vogtle and PSE&G).	No ESPs conducted during FY 2011		

*Change in previously reported FY 2012 target due to resource planning changes.

Review Design Certification Applications on the Schedules Negotiated with the Applicants.

	FY 2008	FY 2009	FY 2010	FY 2011	FY 2012	FY 2013
Target	Complete milestones to support ESBWR and AP 1000 design certification. Begin review of EPR and US APWR design certification application review.	Complete milestones necessary to support ESBWR, EPR and US APWR design certification reviews. Complete review of AP 1000 design certification application.	Complete review of ESBWR design certification application (rulemaking) and AP1000 amended application (rulemaking) and continue review of EPR and APWR design certification applications.	Complete review of ESBWR design certification application (rulemaking) and AP 1000 amended application (rulemaking) and continue review of EPR and APWR design certification applications.	Complete rulemaking activities for AP1000 amendment, and U.S.-ESBWR and U.S.-ABWR AIA amendment. Complete review of EPR design. Begin rulemaking activities for the EPR and the US-APWR.*	Begin review of KEPCO design certification. Complete milestones necessary to support 1 ABWR design certification renewal. Complete rulemaking for EPR and US-APWR.
Actual	Completed milestones to support ESBWR, EPR, and AP 1000 design certification. And the EPR and US APWR design certification application review.	Completed milestones necessary to support the ESBWR, EPR, and US APWR design certifications. Completed milestones associated with ABWR DCA design certification application.	Completed milestones to support U.S.-ESBWR, U.S.-EPR, AP1000 amendment, U.S.-APWR design, and U.S.-ABWR amendment reviews.	Completed review of ESBWR design certification application (rulemaking) and AP 1000 amended application (rulemaking) and continued review of EPR and APWR.		

*Change to previously reported FY 2011 target due to resource planning changes.

Review COL Applications on the Schedules Negotiated with the Applicants.

	FY 2008	FY 2009	FY 2010	FY 2011	FY 2012	FY 2013
Target	Complete milestones associated with conducting 14 COL application reviews.	Complete milestones associated with conducting 20 COL application reviews.	Complete milestones associated with conducting 20 COL application reviews.	Complete milestones associated with conducting 17 COL application reviews.*	Complete milestones associated with conducting 10* continuing COL application.	Complete milestones associated with conducting 10 continuing COL application reviews.
Actual	Completed milestones associated with conducting 14 COL application reviews.	Completed milestones associated with conducting 18 COL application reviews.	Completed milestones associated with conducting 13 COL application reviews.	Completed milestones associated with conducting 12 COL application reviews. ***		

*Change to previously reported FY 2011 target due to resource planning changes.

**Excludes Watts Bar 2 and Bellefonte 1.

***Five of the 17 COLs scheduled for review during FY 2011 remained in a suspended status (outside of NRC's control).

Review Small Modular Reactor (SMR) Design Certification Applications on the Schedules Negotiated with the Applicants.

	FY 2008	FY 2009	FY 2010	FY 2011	FY 2012	FY 2013
Target	New measure in FY 2013.					Complete milestones necessary to support the review of 2 design certification applications.
Actual						

Identify and Resolve Policy and Key Technical Issues Facing the Review of Small Modular Reactor (SMR) Applications. Implement Resolutions Through Rule Changes and/or Guidance Development.

	FY 2008	FY 2009	FY 2010	FY 2011	FY 2012	FY 2013
Target	New measure in FY 2013.					Complete 90% of milestones necessary to support the resolution of policy and key technical issues. In addition, complete 90% of milestones necessary to support implementation of resolutions.
Actual						

Review SMR Pre-Application Submittals on the Schedules Negotiated with the Applicants.

	FY 2008	FY 2009	FY 2010	FY 2011	FY 2012	FY 2013
Target	New measure in FY 2013.					Begin pre-application interactions with prospective DC applicants.
Actual						

Review SMR COL and CP Applications on the Schedules Negotiated with the Applicants.

	FY 2008	FY 2009	FY 2010	FY 2011	FY 2012	FY 2013
Target	New measure in FY 2013.					Complete milestones necessary to support the review of the TVA construction permit application.
Actual						

Oversight

Complete All Vendor Inspections as Scheduled and Resourced

	FY 2008	FY 2009	FY 2010	FY 2011	FY 2012	FY 2013
Target	New measure in FY 2010.		Complete 10 domestic and international vendor inspections.	Complete 15 domestic and international vendor inspections.	Complete 15 domestic and international vendor inspections.	Complete 30 domestic and international vendor inspections.
Actual			Completed 11 vendor inspections, 6 quality assurance implementation inspections, and 3 aircraft impact assessment inspections.	Completed 15 domestic and international vendor inspections.		

Efficiency

	FY 2008	FY 2009	FY 2010	FY 2011	FY 2012	FY 2013
Transistion Subsequent COL Reviews from a 6-Phase to a 4-Phase Approach*.						
Target	New measure in FY 2011.			Level of effort savings is 6 FTE.*	Level of effort savings is 6 FTE.*	Level of effort savings is 6 FTE.
Actual				Data are not available because there has not yet been a complete SCOL review using the 4-phase approach.		

* The projected 6 FTE cost avoidance was factored into the FY 2010 budget. Savings are calculated for a 30-month review period and will allow for process improvements at a rate of 2 FTE per SCOL (averaging 1 FTE per year per SCOL). Nine SCOLs are projected to be reviewed on a
4-phase schedule during FY 2010. This efficiency over the 30-month review period will result in an 18 FTE reduction in budget requests over the 3 year period.

NUCLEAR MATERIALS & WASTE SAFETY

NUCLEAR MATERIALS AND WASTE SAFETY

The Nuclear Materials and Waste Safety Program encompasses the NRC's efforts to ensure that nuclear materials are used and waste is managed in a manner that adequately protects the health and safety of the public, protects the environment, and promotes the common defense and security. Through this program, the NRC regulates uranium processing and fuel facilities; nuclear materials users (medical, industrial, research, academic); spent fuel storage; transportation of radioactive materials; and decontamination and decommissioning of facilities; as well as low-level and high-level radioactive waste. This program contributes to the NRC's Safety and Security goals through activities of the Fuel Facilities, Nuclear Materials Users, Spent Fuel Storage and Transportation, Decommissioning and Low-Level Waste Business Lines, which license and regulate nuclear materials and waste to ensure their safe and secure handling. The Atomic Energy Act of 1954, as amended; the Energy Reorganization Act of 1974, as amended; the Nuclear Waste Policy Act of 1982; and the Energy Policy Act of 2005 are the foundations of the NRC's regulatory authority.

The nuclear fuel cycle process includes extraction of uranium from the ore, conversion of the uranium into a form suitable for enrichment, enrichment of the uranium to a level and type suitable for nuclear fuel, and use of the enriched uranium in fabricating fuel assemblies for use in nuclear reactors. The NRC licenses, oversees, and regulates the facilities involved in the process. Nuclear materials have many industrial, medical, and academic uses outside the nuclear fuel cycle. The NRC licenses, oversees, and regulates large and small users of nuclear materials, such as radiographers, hospitals, private physicians, nuclear gauge users, irradiators, and universities. Licensees with special nuclear material (SNM) verify and document their inventories in the Nuclear Materials Management and Safeguards System (NMMSS) database, which tracks material transfers and inventories. Both the NRC and the Agreement States carry out their respective radiation safety regulatory programs for nuclear materials users under the framework of the National Materials Program (NMP). This covers activities solely carried out by the NRC and 37 Agreement State programs, such as licensing, inspection, response to incidents, staffing and training, and enforcement and investigation.

About three million packages of radioactive materials are shipped each year in the United States by road, rail, air, or water. Regulating the safety of commercial radioactive material shipments is the joint responsibility of the NRC and the U.S. Department of Transportation (DOT). The NRC ensures transportation safety by reviewing and certifying shipping packages for the commercial transport of large quantities of radioactive materials. In addition, the NRC reviews and certifies shipping package designs for the U.S. Department of Energy's (DOE) non-commercial transuranic waste shipments.

The NRC ensures safety and security in the management and disposition of radioactive waste. Nuclear waste is categorized as either low-level radioactive waste (LLW) or high-level radioactive waste (HLW). The NRC and the Agreement States regulate the

NUCLEAR MATERIALS AND WASTE SAFETY STRATEGIC GOALS

Safety—*ensure adequate protection of public health and safety and the environment.*

Security—*ensure adequate protection in the secure use and management of radioactive materials.*

management and disposition of LLW. The NRC or Agreement States license, oversee, and regulate commercial LLW disposal facilities.

The majority of HLW is the irradiated fuel from commercial nuclear power reactors. The NRC licenses, oversees, and regulates the management and disposition of HLW from commercial nuclear power plants and other reactors. Irradiated fuel is initially stored in pools at reactor sites, then after an appropriate time period, it is moved to dry storage. Dry storage is done in casks, or canisters, certified by the NRC for such use. These casks are stored at ISFSIs licensed and regulated by the NRC.

Decommissioning is the safe removal of a nuclear facility from service and reduction of residual radioactivity to a level that permits release of the property and termination of the NRC license. The NRC and Agreement States regulate the decontamination and decommissioning of uranium recovery facilities, materials and fuel cycle facilities, nuclear power plants, and RTRs.

Security efforts in this program include safeguards and security reviews and inspections, force-on-force (FOF) exercises for certain fuel cycle facilities, regulatory improvements, and implementation of a national registry (i.e., the National Source Tracking System (NSTS)) of radioactive sources of concern, and the Integrated Source Management Portfolio (ISMP). The NRC will continue to maintain a high state of incident response readiness and coordination with other Federal, State, and local agencies.

At the time this budget was submitted, the Commission was considering the staff's proposed prioritization of the Fukushima Near-Term Task Force recommendations and regulatory actions to be taken in response to the events at Fukushima Daiichi. The NRC will ensure that regulatory changes necessary to maintain continued safety of domestic nuclear energy will be accommodated and executed.

Nuclear Materials and Waste Safety (Dollars in Millions)						
Business Line	FY 2012 Enacted		FY 2013 Request		Delta FY 2013–FY 2012	
	$M	FTE	$M	FTE	$M	FTE
Fuel Facilities	56.1	228.4	56.1	226.8	0.1	(1.6)
Nuclear Materials Users	93.0	344.7	93.3	341.5	0.3	(3.1)
Spent Fuel Storage & Transportation	40.8	155.1	44.6	162.4	3.8	7.3
Decommissioning & Low-Level Waste	37.3	142.1	38.3	139.3	1.1	(2.8)
High-Level Waste Repository	0.0	0.0	0.0	0.0	0.0	0.0
Total	$227.1	870.4	$232.3	870.1	$5.2	(0.3)

Numbers may not add due to rounding.

The FY 2013 proposed budget request for Nuclear Materials and Waste Safety is $232.3 million, which includes $97.6 million in contract support and travel, and $133.6 million in salaries and benefits to support 870.1 FTE. This would fund activities in Fuel Facilities, Nuclear Materials Users, Spent Fuel Storage and Transportation, and Decommissioning and LLW Business Lines. This funding level represents an increase of $5.2 million, including a decrease of 0.3 FTE, when compared with the FY 2012 enacted budget, which is primarily due to the update of the Waste Confidence (WC) Rule by FY 2019.

	Fuel Facilities by Product Line (Dollars in Millions)					
	FY 2012 Enacted		FY 2013 Request		Delta FY 2013–FY 2012	
Product Line	$M	FTE	$M	FTE	$M	FTE
Licensing	10.8	54.3	9.0	42.1	(1.9)	(12.2)
Oversight	17.8	103.0	19.9	114.3	2.1	11.3
Rulemaking	1.8	8.0	1.3	7.5	(0.5)	(0.5)
Research	0.5	1.4	0.3	1.3	(0.1)	(0.1)
International Activities	1.1	5.1	1.7	9.5	0.5	4.4
Generic HLS	3.1	8.4	2.9	4.3	(0.3)	(4.1)
Event Response	0.6	3.5	0.5	3.2	(0.1)	(0.3)
Subtotal	$35.7	183.6	$35.5	182.1	($0.1)	(1.4)
Corporate Support	20.4	44.9	20.6	44.7	0.2	(0.2)
Total	$56.1	228.4	$56.1	226.8	$0.1	(1.6)

Numbers may not add due to rounding.

FUEL FACILITIES

The Fuel Facilities Business Line activities ensure that fuel cycle facilities are licensed and operated in a manner that adequately protects the health and safety of the public, protects the environment, and promotes the common defense and security. Once uranium ore has been mined and milled (extraction of uranium from the ore), it moves on to conversion, enrichment, and fuel fabrication facilities. Conversion of the uranium changes it into a form suitable for enrichment. Enrichment processes the uranium to a level and type suitable for nuclear fuel and fabrication uses the enriched uranium to make fuel assemblies for nuclear reactors. The NRC licenses, oversees, and regulates fuel cycle facilities, such as conversion, enrichment, and fuel fabrication facilities, as well as research and pilot facilities. There are four uranium enrichment facilities and seven licensed major fuel fabrication and production facilities in the United States.

In FY 2013, the NRC will oversee the construction of the General Electric-Hitachi laser enrichment facility, the AREVA Centrifuge enrichment facility, and the International Isotopes depleted uranium deconversion facility application and will continue conducting Principal Systems, Structures, and Components verifications for the Mixed

Figure 4. U.S. Location of Major U.S. Fuel Cycle Facility Sites

■ Uranium Hexafluoride Conversion Facility (1)
● Uranium Fuel Fabrication Facility (6)
⊗ Mixed Oxide Fuel Fabrication Facility (1)
▲ Gaseous Diffusion Uranium Enrichment Facility (2)
⊿ Gas Centrifuge Uranium Enrichment Facility (3)
△ Laser Separation Enrichment Facility (1)
⊠ Uranium Hexafluoride Deconversion Facility (1)

Licensee	Location	Status
Uranium Hexafluoride Conversion Facility		
Honeywell International, Inc.	Metropolis, IL	active
Uranium Fuel Fabrication Facilities		
Global Nuclear Fuels-Americas, LLC	Wilmington, NC	active
Westinghouse Electric Company, LLC Columbia Fuel Fabrication Facility	Columbia, SC	active
Nuclear Fuel Services, Inc.	Erwin, TN	active
AREVA NP, Inc. Mt. Athos Road Facility	Lynchburg, VA	inactive—possession only
B&W Nuclear Operations Group	Lynchburg, VA	active
AREVA NP, Inc.	Richland, WA	active
Mixed Oxide Fuel Fabrication Facility		
Shaw AREVA MOX Services, LLC	Aiken, SC	in construction, operating license under review
Gaseous Diffusion Uranium Enrichment Facilities		
USEC Inc.	Paducah, KY	active
USEC Inc.	Piketon, OH	in cold shutdown*
Gas Centrifuge Uranium Enrichment Facilities		
USEC Inc.	Piketon, OH	in construction
Louisiana Energy Services (URENCO-USA)	Eunice, NM	active**
AREVA Enrichment Services	Idaho Falls, ID	under review
Laser Separation Enrichment Facility		
GE-Hitachi	Wilmington, NC	under review
Uranium Hexafluoride Deconversion Facility		
International Isotopes	Hobbes, NM	under review

*Currently in cold shutdown and in process of decertification and not used for enrichment.
**Partially operating and producing enriched uranium while undergoing further phases of construction.
Note: The NRC regulates nine other facilities that possess significant quantities of special nuclear material (other than reactors) or process source material (other than uranium recovery facilities). Data as of April 2011.

Oxide (MOX) Fuel Fabrication Facility. The NRC will continue to oversee the operation of the other fuel cycle facilities.

Licensed fuel facilities possess Spent Nuclear Material (SNM), such as plutonium and enriched uranium. These SNM licensees verify and document their inventories in the Nuclear Material Management and Safeguard System (NMMSS) database. In addition to tracking inventories, the database tracks material transfers.

Fuel facilities activities include the Nuclear Materials Information Program (NMIP) and the interagency agreement with Department of Energy (DOE) for certification and accreditation of classified computer systems at enrichment facilities. Other activities include environmental, emergency preparedness, and licensee performance reviews; legal advice and representation; adjudicatory hearing-related activities; independent review and advice; security support for licensing activities; inspection oversight; allegations and enforcement activities; rulemaking; international cooperation and assistance; International Atomic Energy Agency missions; export and import licensing; and treaties, agreements, and conventions.

The NRC has organized fuel facilities activities into product lines that best support Safety and Security strategies and accomplish strategic outcomes as they relate to fuel cycle facilities. The resources requested support all direct aspects of fuel facilities within the following seven product lines: Licensing, Oversight, Rulemaking, Research, International Activities, Generic Homeland Security, and Event Response.

The outputs of the product lines under this business line contribute to the scoring of the NRC Safety and Security Performance Measures and their contribution to the achievement of its Strategic Outcomes.

Changes from FY 2012 Enacted Budget

Resources remain the same for the overall business line, but workload shifted within the product lines. For example, resources decrease with respect to the Licensing Product Line to reflect the completion of existing license application reviews, as well as a reduced level of effort for developing the regulatory infrastructure for licensing of reprocessing facilities. Resources increase in the Oversight Product Line to support significant construction activities.

Licensing

For FY 2013, the NRC requests $9.0 million, including 42.1 FTE, for licensing activities. This represents a funding decrease of $1.9 million, including 12.2 FTE, when compared with the FY 2012 enacted budget. This decrease is due to the completion of existing license applications and issuance of licenses.

The Licensing Product Line supports licensing fuel cycle facilities (such as uranium conversion, enrichment, and fuel fabrication) and research and pilot facilities. The workload includes performing reviews of licensing actions, adjudicatory hearing-related activities, independent review and advice, legal advice and representation for the MOX Fuel Fabrication Facility, International Isotopes depleted uranium deconversion facility, one medical isotope application, construction activities for U.S. Enrichment Corporation (USEC), AREVA-Idaho, General Electric-Hitachi, AREVA-Lynchburg, Nuclear Fuel Services, and Louisiana Energy Services (LES). Funding

Strategic Goal Strategies Supported by Licensing

Safety—*develop, maintain, and implement licensing and regulatory programs for fuel facilities material, spent fuel management, waste management, uranium recovery, and decommissioning.*

Security—*review security plans and changes for consistency with security requirements.*

is requested for environmental aspects of the mandatory hearing for General Electric-Hitachi and for environmental assessments of other licensing actions. Funding also supports the performance of emergency preparedness licensing reviews, security-related licensing activities and revision of the fuel cycle aspects of reactor environmental reports, and associated environmental impact statements.

Licensing confirms that requests for new facilities and existing licensee requests for license renewals and amendments are consistent with the NRC's rules and regulations to ensure the adequate protection of public health and safety, protect the environment, and promote the common defense and security.

Oversight

For FY 2013, the NRC requests $19.9 million, including 114.3 FTE, for oversight activities. This represents a funding increase of $2.1 million, including 11.3 FTE, when compared with the FY 2012 enacted budget. This increase is due to increased oversight to support significant construction activities.

The Oversight Product Line supports baseline and reactive inspections at fuel cycle facilities and support of oversight activities with technical and licensing expertise, allegations and enforcement activities, licensee performance reviews, enhancing the fuel cycle oversight process, and supporting Force-on-Force (FOF) activities. The workload includes construction oversight for the MOX Fuel Fabrication Facility with increased effort on principal structures, systems, and components and continuation of safety-related construction for AREVA, General Electric-Hitachi, and International Isotopes. LES continues to request a new cascade every 6 to 8 weeks with associated readiness reviews. LES and USEC/American Centrifuge Plant (ACP) construction/operational readiness review inspections continue. The workload includes security baseline and FOF inspections, reinspections, and followup for facilities that possess Category I quantities of SNM. The workload also includes the installation of resident inspectors at GE-Hitachi, USEC/ACP, and International Isotopes facilities.

NRC oversight continuously ensures the safe and secure operation of currently licensed fuel cycle facilities and identifies significant performance issues. The oversight process ensures that licensees take appropriate actions to maintain acceptable safety and security operating performance which ensure the adequate protection of the public health and safety, protect the environment, and promote the common defense and security. The oversight process also ensures that facilities under construction are built in accordance with NRC requirements.

Rulemaking

For FY 2013, the NRC requests $1.3 million, including 7.5 FTE, for rulemaking activities. This represents a funding decrease of $0.5 million, including 0.5 FTE, when compared with the FY 2012 enacted budget. This decrease is due to a reduced level of effort for developing the regulatory infrastructure for licensing reprocessing facilities.

The Rulemaking Product Line provides support for the high-priority and medium-priority rulemakings in FY 2013. The workload includes the final rule development activities for 10 CFR Part 74, "Material Control and Accounting of Special Nuclear Material Rulemaking" (the final rule will be sent to the Commission in April 2012). Funding also supports rulemaking in security-related areas for enhanced security at fuel cycle facilities (CAT I, II, III, gaseous diffusion plant), material categorization, 10 CFR Part 26, "Fitness-For-Duty Programs," and fingerprinting for Safeguards Information access, which will update security regulations to be consistent with orders and licensing commitments at fuel cycle facilities. Resources will also support progress in the development of the reprocessing regulatory framework.

Research

For FY 2013, the NRC requests $0.3 million, including 1.3 FTE, for research activities. This represents essentially no change in funding, when compared with the FY 2012 enacted budget, which does not represent a significant change in workload.

The Research Product Line supports the NRC's regulatory mission by providing technical advice, tools, and information to identify and resolve safety issues and make regulatory decisions. This includes conducting confirmatory experiments and analyses and preparing the agency for the future by evaluating the safety aspects of new technologies.

The workload includes support for the review of fuel facility applications and enhancements of review guidance for geologic, seismic, structural, external events, instrumentation and control, and human factors aspects of the application as requested in the user need.

Resources also support a long-term research project related to advanced reprocessing. This project would address the differences in technology associated with nonaqueous reprocessing as a scoping effort to identify topics for more detailed investigation.

STRATEGIC GOAL STRATEGIES SUPPORTED BY RULEMAKING

Safety—maintain a framework of rules, regulatory guidance, and standard review plans that promote licensee compliance with underlying safety principles.

Security—use a risk-informed approach to implement appropriate regulatory controls for the possession, handling, import, export, and transshipment of radioactive materials.

STRATEGIC GOAL STRATEGIES SUPPORTED BY RESEARCH

Safety—improve the NRC's regulatory programs and apply safety-focused research to anticipate and resolve safety issues.

Security—use research to inform the security activities of the agency.

Safety—*use international collaboration and coordination to inform decisionmaking.*

Security—*promote U.S. national security interests and nuclear proliferation policy objectives for NRC-licensed imports and exports of source and special nuclear materials and nuclear equipment.*

STRATEGIC GOAL STRATEGIES SUPPORTED BY GENERIC HOMELAND SECURITY

Safety—*conduct NRC safety, security, and emergency preparedness programs in an integrated manner.*

Security—*support Federal response plans that employ an approach to the security of nuclear facilities and radioactive material that integrates the efforts of licensees and Federal, State, local, and Tribal authorities.*

International Activities

For FY 2013, the NRC requests $1.7 million, including 9.5 FTE, for international activities. This represents a funding increase of $0.5 million, including 4.4 FTE, when compared with the FY 2012 enacted budget, which does not represent a significant change in workload.

The International Activities Product Line supports NRC work with international counterparts to exchange information, expertise, operating experiences, and ongoing research to recognize and respond to emerging technical issues and promote best safety and security practices. In FY 2013, the International Activities work includes multilateral cooperation and assistance; support for IAEA missions; export and import licensing; and international treaties, agreements, and conventions.

Generic Homeland Security

In FY 2013, the NRC requests $2.9 million, including 4.3 FTE, for generic homeland security activities. This represents a funding decrease of $0.3 million, including 4.1 FTE, when compared with the FY 2012 enacted budget, which does not represent a significant change in workload.

The Generic Homeland Security Product Line supports security activities related to intergovernmental coordination and communication, including activities associated with the development of counterintelligence programs. It also supports homeland security activities that are not licensee specific.

The workload includes support for the NMMSS database operations, the Defense Tracking Technical System, and the NMIP. Funding supports the review of new safeguards technologies, intergovernmental coordination and communication of homeland security matters, and international security-related activities. Funding also supports homeland security travel-related activities for intergovernmental coordination, cooperation, and communication of homeland security matters related to fuel cycle facilities.

Event Response

In FY 2013, the NRC requests $0.5 million, including 3.2 FTE, for event response activities. This represents a funding decrease of $0.1 million, including 0.3 FTE, when compared with the FY 2012 enacted budget, which does not represent a significant change in workload.

The Event Response Product Line supports efforts to enhance the fuel facilities event response program, plans, and procedures.

The workload includes support for one full-participation emergency preparedness exercise with an operating fuel cycle facility. Funding also supports development and maintenance of the response capability associated with fuel cycle facility-related incidents (i.e., emergency response coordinators, a training and qualification program, procedures, interagency and interagency coordination, and outreach). Funding also supports regional incident response actions for fuel cycle facility licensees, including maintenance of a response capability for fuel cycle facility-related incidents.

Significant Accomplishments in FY 2011

The NRC continued its safety, security, and environmental reviews of two license applications for uranium enrichment facilities. These facilities increase the concentration of the uranium 235 isotope from its natural enrichment of about 0.7 percent of natural uranium to 4 to 5 percent. The uranium is used in commercial power reactors, such as those used throughout the commercial power industry in the United States. The first application, submitted in December 2008 by AREVA, is for a centrifuge enrichment facility to be built near Idaho Falls, ID. The second, submitted in June 2009 by General Electric-Hitachi, is for a laser-based enrichment facility to be built in Wilmington, NC.

The agency reviewed the AREVA Enrichment Services Eagle Rock license application for the Eagle Rock Enrichment Facility. The agency found the record sufficient and the staff review adequate to support findings for license approval related to 10 CFR Parts 30, 40, and 70. The staff held the evidentiary hearing for the final environmental impact statement in July 2011 in Idaho Falls, ID.

In December 2010, the agency approved the issuance of the final safety evaluation report for the license application by Shaw AREVA MOX Services, LLC, to possess and use radioactive material at the Mixed-Oxide Fuel Fabrication Facility at DOE's Savannah River Site near Aiken, SC.

In response to sustained industry interest in reprocessing spent nuclear fuel, the NRC continued developing a technical basis for rulemaking to establish the regulatory framework for licensing a reprocessing facility. During FY 2011, the agency continued resolving the identified gaps and establishing an effective and efficient regulatory framework.

The NRC completed more than 120 licensing actions for operating fuel facilities, including the following:

> Completed the review to terminate the Portsmouth Gaseous Diffusion Plant Certificate

> Issued a new license for Oregon State University

> Issued the license renewal for Idaho State University License

> Issued a new license to receive, possess, inspect, and store fresh fuel assemblies at the Watts Bar Nuclear Plan Unit 2

STRATEGIC GOAL STRATEGIES SUPPORTED BY EVENT RESPONSE

Safety—*effectively respond to events at NRC-licensed facilities and other events of national interest, including maintaining and enhancing the NRC's critical incident response and communication capabilities.*

Security—*support Federal response plans that employ an approach to the security of nuclear facilities and radioactive material that integrates the efforts of licensees and Federal, State, local, and Tribal authorities.*

Fuel Facilities Output Measures

Licensing

Timeliness Of Completing "Complex" Fuel Cycle Licensing Actions, from the Date of Acceptance, Excluding Request for Additional Information with an Assumption of 30-Day Response to a Request for Additional Information.					
	FY 2008	FY 2009	FY 2010	FY 2011	FY 2012	FY 2013
Target:	New measure to begin in FY 2010		100% ≤ 1.5 yrs.	100% ≤ 1.5 yrs.	100% < 1.5 yrs	100% < 1.5 yrs.
Actual:			100% ≤ 1.5 yrs.	98% ≤ 1.5 yrs*		

Timeliness of Completing "Non-Complex" Fuel Cycle Licensing Actions (E.G., Amendments And Reviews) from the Date Of Acceptance, Including a 30-Day Response for a Request for Additional Information.					
	FY 2008	FY 2009	FY 2010	FY 2011	FY 2012	FY 2013
Target:	New measure to begin in FY 2010		85% ≤ 150 days 100% < 1 year	85% ≤ 150 days 100% < 1 year	85% ≤ 150 days 100% < 1 year	85% ≤ 150 days 100% < 1 year
Actual:			92% ≤ 150 days 100% < 1 year	92% ≤ 150 days 100% < 1 year		

Oversight

Timeliness in Completing Reviewsfor Technical Allegations					
	FY 2008	FY 2009	FY 2010	FY 2011	FY 2012	FY 2013
Target:	90% < 150 days 95% < 180 days 100% < 360 days	90% ≤ 150 days 95% ≤ 180 days 100% ≤ 360 days	90% ≤ 150 days 95% ≤ 180 days 100% ≤ 360 days	90% ≤ 150 days 95% ≤ 180 days 100% ≤ 360 days	90% < 150 days 95% < 180 days 100% < 360 days	90% < 150 days 95% < 180 days 100% < 360 days
Actual:	100% ≤ 150 days 100% ≤ 180 days 100% ≤ 360 days	100% ≤ 150 days 100% ≤ 180 days 100% ≤ 360 days	81% ≤ 150 days* 96% ≤ 180 days 100% ≤ 360 days	97% ≤ 150 days, 98% ≤ 180 days 100% ≤ 360 days		

*This metric was not met because allegations in the first quarter were not being closed in ≤ 150 days. Three of the four were affected by regional staff reassignments and case complexities requiring substantial review by staff and management. The fourth case involved issues of dual regulation between the NRC and the U.S. Environmental Protection Agency (EPA) and required extensive research of EPA requirements and communications with State representatives. The Region focused attention in this area throughout the remainder of FY 2010 (closed all but one fuel facility allegation in the second and third quarters in ≤ 150 days), but was ultimately unable to meet the metric, primarily due to the considerable staff and management effort required to evaluate three new fuel facility allegations in the fourth quarter of FY 2010 that each involved unusually large numbers of concerns, causing the time needed for closure to be > 150 (but < 180) days.

Safety and Safeguards Inspection Modules. Complete All Core and Reactive Inspection Modules as Scheduled in Fuel Cycle Master Inspection Plan.					
	FY 2008	FY 2009	FY 2010	FY 2011	FY 2012	FY 2013
Target:	Complete 266 inspection modules.	Complete 286 inspection modules.	Complete 286 inspection modules.	Complete 328 inspection modules.*	Complete 307 inspection modules.*	Measure discontinued in FY 2013.
Actual:	Completed 269 inspection modules.	Completed 286 inspection modules.	Completed 289 inspection modules.	Completed 320 inspection modules.**		

*USEC/ACP commenced enrichment operations during FY 2010. LES is not expected to commence operations until after FY 2012.
**An material control and accounting inspection scheduled for LES in February that was postponed to coincide with upcoming readiness review inspections; a low-enriched NFS inspection scheduled for July moved to October to coincide with the high-enriched inspection; and the fact that an LES inspection report not issued in this FY to resolve a nonconcurrence. Since the inspection program is conducted by calendar year (CY), postponement of the MC&A LES and Nuclear Fuel Services, Inc. inspections to FY12 Q1 (while still in CY 2011 inspection year) will support completion of the core program.

Timeliness of Safety and Safeguards Inspection Modules. Complete Core Inspection Modules as Scheduled in Fuel Cycle Master Inspection Plan						
	FY 2008	FY 2009	FY 2010	FY 2011	FY 2012	FY 2013
Target:	>97% completed on time.	>97% completed on time.	>97% completed on time.	>99% completed on time.	>99% completed on time.	Measure discontinued in FY 2013.
Actual:	100% completed on time.	100% completed on time.	100% completed on time.	100% completed on time.		

Percentage of Operating Facilities for Which the Core Inspection Program Was Completed During the Most Recently Ended Inspection Cycle. *						
	FY 2008	FY 2009	FY 2010	FY 2011	FY 2012	FY 2013
Target:	New measure in FY 2013					100%
Actual:						

*Replaces former output measures on core and reactive inspection modules and timeliness of safety and safeguards inspection modules.

Efficiency

New Fuel Facilities Hearing Support*						
	FY 2008	FY 2009	FY 2010	FY 2011	FY 2012	FY 2013
Target:			New efficiency measure to begin in FY 2011	Actual hours expended on major tasks in support of licensing board hearings as documented in the Fuel Cycle Safety and Safeguards Division Operating Plan will not exceed the projected hours by more than 10 percent.*	Actual hours expended on major tasks in support of licensing board hearings as documented in the Fuel Cycle Safety and Safeguards Division Operating Plan will not exceed the projected hours by more than 10 percent.*	Actual hours expended on major tasks in support of licensing board hearings as documented in the Fuel Cycle Safety and Safeguards Division Operating Plan will not exceed the projected hours by more than 10 percent.*

Actual:

*Targets, baselines, and calculation methods are under development and measure may be revised.

NUCLEAR MATERIALS USERS

	Nuclear Materials Users by Product Line (Dollars in Millions)					
	FY 2012 Enacted		FY 2013 Request		Delta FY 2013–FY 2012	
Product Line	$M	FTE	$M	FTE	$M	FTE
Licensing	13.4	67.1	13.0	65.9	(0.4)	(1.2)
Oversight	19.4	99.2	19.2	97.2	(0.2)	(2.0)
Rulemaking	3.7	20.3	3.5	18.9	(0.2)	(1.4)
Research	1.0	4.1	1.2	4.0	0.2	(0.1)
International Activities	2.1	12.0	2.5	13.9	0.3	2.0
Generic HLS	15.5	33.8	15.3	31.5	(0.1)	(2.3)
Event Response	0.9	5.1	0.8	4.9	(0.0)	(0.2)
State, Tribal & Federal Programs	7.2	37.3	7.6	39.6	0.4	2.3
Subtotal	**$63.2**	**278.9**	**$63.1**	**276.0**	**($0.0)**	**(2.9)**
Corporate Support	29.8	65.7	30.2	65.5	0.3	(0.2)
Total	$93.0	344.7	$93.3	341.5	$0.3	(3.1)

Numbers may not add due to rounding.

Nuclear materials have many industrial, medical, and academic uses. The NRC licenses, oversees, and regulates large and small users of nuclear materials, such as radiographers, hospitals, private physicians, nuclear gauge users, irradiators, and universities.

Nuclear Materials Users activities support the licensing, inspection, event evaluation, research, incident response, allegation, enforcement, and rulemaking to maintain the regulatory safety and security infrastructure needed to process and handle nuclear materials. The agency's safety activities include completion of approximately 2,500 materials licensing actions and 1,000 routine health and safety inspections. The NRC also works on approximately 20–25 active materials and waste rulemakings.

The Agreement State program has been in existence since 1959 with the adoption of Section 274 of the Atomic Energy Act (AEA). At present, there are 37 Agreement States. Under Section 274 of the AEA, the NRC has programmatic oversight responsibility to periodically review the actions of the Agreement States to ensure compliance with the requirements of the AEA to maintain adequate and compatible programs. The current review process under the Integrated Materials Performance Evaluation Program (IMPEP) is conducted with State staff participation.

Nuclear Materials Users activities include reviews and issuance of NRC import/export authorizations, materials-related wrongdoing investigations, adjudicatory hearings for materials licensing and enforcement proceedings, technical training, and continuous improvements and centralized oversight of information technology and information management.

Nuclear Materials Users security activities include the implementation and operation of a national registry of radioactive sources of concern to improve controls on risk-significant radioactive materials to prevent their malevolent use. The ISMP contract is in the process of integrating the three core systems consisting of the NSTS, Web-Based Licensing (WBL), and the License Verification System (LVS) that will license and track sources and other radioactive materials under one management mechanism. Further, security activities include conducting inspections of increased controls at materials facilities; security inspections of irradiators, manufacturers, and distributors; inspections of radioactive materials in quantities of concern; and prelicensing inspections of new materials applicants. All of these activities strengthen controls for the possession, handling, import, and export of nuclear materials. In addition, resources will be used to conduct NRC's Agreement State liaison activities regarding enhanced control and security actions for materials licensees, as well as cooperative efforts and liaison with all State and local governments and Native American Tribal governments, in matters related to homeland security for nuclear waste and materials.

The NRC has organized Nuclear Materials Users activities into product lines that best support safety and security strategies and affect strategic outcomes as they relate to materials licensing, inspection, and Agreement State activities. The resources requested support all direct aspects of Nuclear Materials Users within the following eight product lines: Licensing; Oversight; Rulemaking; Research; International Activities; Generic Homeland Security; Event Response; and State, Tribal, and Federal Programs. The efforts under Nuclear Materials Users are designed to ensure that nuclear materials are licensed and used in a manner that adequately protects health and safety of the public, protects the environment, and promotes the common defense and security

The outputs of the product lines under this business line contribute to the scoring of the NRC Safety and Security Performance Measures and their contribution to the achievement of its Strategic Outcomes.

Changes from FY 2012 Enacted Budget

Resources increased in the Generic Homeland Security Product Line as a result of a comparability adjustment from the Licensing Product Line for better alignment of ISMP resources.

Licensing

For FY 2013, the NRC requests $13.0 million, including 65.9 FTE, for licensing activities. This represents a funding decrease of $0.4 million, including a decrease of 1.2 FTE, when compared with the FY 2012 enacted budget, which does not represent a significant change in workload.

The Licensing Product Line supports completion of approximately 2,500 materials licensing actions (new applications, amendments, renewals, and terminations) in FY 2013. It is anticipated that materials licensing receipts will remain level and the agency will be able to continue implementing the recommendations for enhanced security for licensing. Licensing confirms that requests to use nuclear materials or modify existing uses provide an adequate margin of safety and security consistent with the NRC's rules and regulations to ensure the adequate protection of public health and safety, protect the environment, and promote the common defense and security. Resources are also budgeted over the planning period for legal assistance supporting materials licensing. In FY 2013, the agency supports adjudicatory hearing-related activities and limited appearance sessions for materials licensing proceedings. Legal

STRATEGIC GOAL STRATEGIES SUPPORTED BY LICENSING

Safety—develop, maintain, and implement licensing and regulatory programs for fuel facilities, materials, spent fuel management, waste management, uranium recovery, and decommissioning activities.

Security—support Federal response plans that employ an approach to the security of nuclear facilities and radioactive material that integrates the efforts of licensees, Federal, State, local, and Tribal authorities.

advice and counsel will support materials licensing and enforcement actions based on new security requirements affecting materials licensees.

Oversight

For FY 2013, the NRC requests $19.2 million, including 97.2 FTE, for oversight activities. This represents a funding decrease of $0.2 million along with a decrease of 2.0 FTE, when compared with the FY 2012 enacted budget, which does not represent a significant change in workload.

The Oversight Product Line activities provide for the continued safe and secure use of nuclear materials. These activities provide the means to identify significant issues and ensure that licensees take appropriate actions to maintain acceptable levels of safety and security in their operating procedures, performance, and the use of nuclear materials. Oversight includes resources for inspections, event evaluations, allegations, investigations, enforcement, and related activities associated with the management and oversight of nuclear materials.

The workload includes completion of approximately 1,000 routine health and safety inspections in FY 2013, as well as reciprocity and reactive inspections, and a registration and followup inspection program for certain general licensees. Resources will support implementation of the recommendation from the materials working group and the external independent review working group to revise the licensing and inspection infrastructure. The agency will support investigations of wrongdoing, materials-related enforcement actions, oversight of the Alternative Dispute Resolution (ADR) and allegation programs, and external safety culture program activities.

The resources support event and incident evaluation activities, which include the protective measures team emergency response support function, as well as the orphan source activity, and funding for the Nuclear Materials Events Database.

Continued coordination with States on agreements, as authorized by Section 274i of the Atomic Energy Act of 1954, and homeland security are planned. These activities include support for development and distribution of advisories, development and implementation of additional security measures (e.g., development of implementing guidance), and ensuring that other homeland security information is provided to authorized State and local government officials. The agency will continue to develop, coordinate, and assist in the maintenance of Section 274i agreements with States to conduct security inspections on behalf of the NRC for NRC-issued security orders.

Rulemaking

For FY 2013, the NRC requests $3.5 million, including 18.9 FTE, for rulemaking activities. This represents a funding decrease of $0.2 million, including a decrease of 1.4 FTE, when compared with the FY 2012 enacted budget, which does not represent a significant change in workload.

The Rulemaking Product Line will support rulemaking activities, including legal support to maintain the regulatory infrastructure needed to process and handle nuclear materials. Rules, guidance, and regulations promote licensee compliance with underlying safety principles and requirements.

Rulemaking support activities decrease slightly. In FY 2013, approximately 20-25 active materials and waste safety rulemakings will be worked on, as well as continued interactive liaison with industry and professional societies to develop new codes and consensus standards and to address petitions for rulemaking submitted to the agency. Examples of rulemakings determined as high priority are amendments under 10 CFR Part 35, "'Medical Use of Byproduct Material", and 10 CFR Part 71, "Packaging and Transportation of Radioactive Material," and compatibility with IAEA transportation standards. Rulemaking resources systematically improve the NRC's regulatory program to ensure the safe use and management of nuclear materials and to resolve safety issues. They also improve the NRC's regulations by adding needed requirements, eliminating unnecessary requirements, and minimizing jurisdictional overlaps. The NRC will continue to work on the highest priority rulemakings.

International Activities

For FY 2013, the NRC requests $2.5 million, including 13.9 FTE, for international activities. This represents a funding increase of $0.3 million, including 2.0 FTE, when compared with the FY 2012 enacted budget, which does not represent a significant change in workload.

The International Activities Product Line increases slightly to support NRC reviews and decisions on import/export authorizations of nuclear components and radiological materials, Executive Branch Subsequent Arrangements and Proposed 810 Licenses, control and tracking of imports and exports of sources, and bilateral and multilateral activities initiated for the exchange of technical information for the safe handling, storage, transport, and disposal of nuclear waste. Resources also provide for assistance activities related to the safety and security of medical and industrial sources, support to the IAEA missions related to training and regulation of nuclear materials, and assistance to foreign regulatory bodies through the assignee program.

The International Activities Product Line provides the means to work with international counterparts to exchange information, expertise, operating experience, and ongoing research to recognize and respond to emerging technical issues and promote best safety and security practices. The NRC also participates in the development of international standards to ensure they are soundly based and to determine whether substantial safety and security improvements can be identified and incorporated domestically.

Research

For FY 2013, the NRC requests $1.2 million, including 4.0 FTE, for research activities. This represents a funding increase of $0.2 million, including a decrease of 0.1 FTE, when compared to the FY 2012 enacted budget, which does not represent a significant change in workload.

The Research Product Line supports activities to identify, lead, or sponsor reviews that support the resolution of ongoing and future safety issues, including providing tools and expertise needed to support the NRC's independent decisionmaking process.

The Research Product Line supports research on the development of human reliability analysis informed tools to assist NRC staff involved with the review and inspection of medical applications of byproduct materials, as well as continuing research on

STRATEGIC GOAL STRATEGIES SUPPORTED BY INTERNATIONAL ACTIVITIES

Safety—use domestic and international collaboration and cooperation to inform decisionmaking.

Security—promote U.S. national security interests and nuclear proliferation policy objectives for NRC-licensed imports and exports of source and special nuclear materials and nuclear equipment.

STRATEGIC GOAL STRATEGIES SUPPORTED BY RESEARCH

Safety—improve the NRC's regulatory programs and apply safety-focused research to anticipate and resolve safety issues.

Security—use research to inform the security activities of the agency.

gemstone irradiation and consumer products. In addition, research for the medical and industrial sectors will support development and alignment of radiation protection regulations and guidance with the 2007 International Commission on Radiological Protection recommendations.

Generic Homeland Security

For FY 2013, the NRC requests $15.3 million, including 31.5 FTE, for generic homeland security activities. This represents a funding decrease of $0.1 million, including a decrease of 2.3 FTE, when compared with the FY 2012 enacted budget, which does not represent a significant change in workload.

The Generic Homeland Security Product Line supports security coordination and liaison, security rulemaking activities, including legal support for the homeland security regulatory improvements initiatives, control and tracking of imports and exports of sources, homeland security travel funds, and the development and implementation of the ISMP.

The resources are for liaison activities related to security activities that support NRC policy interactions at the IAEA and the NEA on security and safety issues, consultations on security standards, rulemakings, and intergovernmental coordination. Resources also support

high-priority security rulemakings. The resources are also budgeted for the ISMP development, which will integrate the three systems (NSTS, WBL, and LVS) that license and track sources and radioactive materials under one management mechanism. This development effort is vital to forming a comprehensive national materials license repository. The near-term results in FY 2013 will be the first full year of operation of WBL and LVS, and the overall results will be enhanced control and accountability of radioactive materials.

Event Response

For FY 2013, the NRC requests $0.8 million, including 4.9 FTE, to provide for event response activities. This represents no increase in funding, including a decrease of 0.2 FTE, when compared with the FY 2012 enacted budget, which does not represent a significant change in workload.

The Event Response Product Line provides the means to effectively respond to events involving nuclear materials, including maintaining and enhancing the NRC's critical event response and communication capabilities. In FY 2013, the budget for the Event Response Product Line remains essentially flat to support event response actions for materials licensees, including the maintenance of a 24/7 response capability for materials-related incidents.

State, Tribal, and Federal Programs

For FY 2013, the NRC requests $7.6 million, including 39.6 FTE, for State, Tribal, and Federal Programs. This represents a funding increase of $0.4 million, including 2.3 FTE, when compared with the FY 2012 enacted budget, which reflects a slight increase for coordination and liaison with states and local governments, Federal agencies, Native American Tribal governments, and interstate organizations on policy and notifications of interest for nuclear waste and materials.

The State, Tribal, and Federal Programs Product Line conducts materials activities related to Agreement States, including oversight, technical assistance, and cooperative efforts. Together, the NRC and Agreement States regulate more than 22,000 specific and 150,000 general licenses.

This product line supports the cooperative activities with Agreement States and the conduct of periodic reviews of Agreement State programs to ensure they are adequate to protect public health and safety and that are compatible with NRC programs. Resources provide for conducting materials activities related to Agreement States and liaison, including oversight, technical assistance, cooperative efforts, and enhanced control and security actions for materials licensees. Resources also fund NRC-sponsored Agreement State training and travel activities.

FY 2013 budgetary resources support the continued implementation of the Agreement State program. The resources provide support to conduct IMPEP reviews (10–12), outreach to potential new Agreement States and process new agreements (1), process Agreement State incidents/events (50), participate in and coordinate State participation in regulatory development, coordinate and fund State participation in NRC training courses, respond to State technical assistance requests, respond to and coordinate responses to allegations about Agreement State licensees or regulatory programs, interact with the Conference of Radiation Control Program Directors, Inc., and the Organization of Agreement States, Inc., and develop and maintain policies and procedures for the program. This activity includes the statutory requirement for the NRC to make a determination that all applicable standards and requirements have been met prior to a uranium milling license termination by the Agreement State, and alternate 11e.(2) standards are adequate before they are implemented by the Agreement State (1 or 2 cases per year).

The NRC also coordinates with Agreement States in the waste area on LLW and decommissioning since all currently operating LLW sites are located in Agreement States. These activities provide public confidence and assurance that the Agreement States are conducting adequate and compatible programs.

This product line provides for the Materials State, Federal, and Tribal Liaison Program that informs, notifies, and coordinates with Governor-appointed representatives, other Federal agencies, and Native American Tribal governments on matters involving the NRC. This outreach enhances public confidence in the national program and collects input from NRC stakeholders. Consistent with Executive Order 13175, "Consultation and Coordination with Indian Tribal Governments, dated November 6, 2000," the NRC has adopted agency practices that ensure consultation and cooperation with Tribal governments. For example, the NRC interacts with Native American Tribal governments on nuclear-related regulatory issues that include uranium recovery

STRATEGIC GOAL STRATEGIES SUPPORTED BY STATE, TRIBAL, AND FEDERAL PROGRAMS

Safety—ccontinue to support Agreement States in developing, maintaining, and implementing licensing and regulatory programs for materials users.

Security—share security information with appropriate stakeholders and international partners.

licensing and long-term strategies for remediation, reactor licensing and inspection activities, reactor license renewal, and nuclear waste transportation and disposal. The NRC is currently in the process of implementing an internal protocol for government-to-government interaction with Tribal governments in response to Commission direction. Recently, NRC rulemaking efforts to provide Native American Tribes with advance notification of high-level waste shipments across Tribal lands has required the agency to provide resources to Tribal outreach and communication with all 564 Federally recognized tribes to solicit comments on this activity.

Significant Accomplishments in FY 2011

The NRC completed 2,104 materials licensing actions and 1,010 routine health and safety inspections in FY 2011. The agency maintained its high standards with timely reviews of nuclear material license renewals and sealed-source and device designs in FY 2011. The agency completed 97 percent of new application and license amendment reviews within 90 days of receipt and 97 percent of license renewal and sealed-source and device design reviews within 180 days of receipt.

The NRC proposed to amend its regulations that govern the licensing and distribution of byproduct materials aimed at making regulations clearer, more risk-informed, and up-to-date in FY 2011. In addition, an agency Working Group began to prepare a 10 CFR Part 35 medical proposed rule for public comment, which is expected to be published in the Federal Register in FY 2013. The rule proposes the following changes in 10 CFR Part 35: modifying preceptor attestation requirements; extending grandfathering to certified individuals that were named in Part 35 prior to October 25, 2005; naming associate or assistant Radiation Safety Officers on an NRC medical-use license; and a likely change in the definition of a medical event, including revised reporting and notifications of medical events for permanent implant brachytherapy. The agency also conducted a special series of facilitated public workshops to engage stakeholders on possible revisions of the agency's radiation protection requirements in light of international recommendations.

The NRC continued its efforts to mitigate the potential risk of terrorist threats through enhanced security and controls for the use, storage, and transportation of risk-significant byproduct material and spent nuclear fuel. In collaboration with the Department of Homeland Security (DHS), DOE, and other Federal, State, and local agencies, the NRC continued to assess the potential use of risk-significant sources in radiological dispersal devices and to coordinate efforts to enhance radioactive source protection and security. The NRC also worked with Agreement States to implement requirements for licensees that enhance the security and control of risk-significant radioactive material, including development of an inspection program to verify the implementation of these measures.

The NRC staff participated in activities related to the Government Coordinating Council, which enables interagency and cross-jurisdictional coordination on critical infrastructure and key resources, including transportation and material security. The staff also participated in trilateral meetings with DHS and the National Nuclear Security Administration to coordinate resolution of issues related to radioactive material security.

The NRC also implemented the National Source Tracking Rule, which requires licensees to report information on the possession of IAEA Category 1 and 2 radioactive sources (i.e., nationally tracked sources). The rule requires NRC and Agreement State licensees to report transactions involving the manufacture, transfer, receipt, disassembly, and disposal of nationally tracked sources. In FY 2011, licensees completed the second annual inventory reconciliation of their nationally tracked sources.

The NSTS, WBL, and LVS, are key components of a comprehensive program for the security and control of radioactive material called the ISMP. WBL's database will serve as a national license data warehouse and will have the capacity to maintain information on all U.S. licensees. NSTS maintains over 70,000 risk-significant radioactive sources possessed by approximately 1,400 licensees. The ISMP will provide licensees, regulators, and Federal agencies with an additional round-the-clock means of determining the legitimacy of individuals possessing or seeking to obtain radioactive material to ensure that the materials are obtained only in authorized amounts by legitimate users.

Nuclear Material Users Output Measures

Licensing

Timeliness of Licensing Actions-Review of Application for New Materials Licenses and License Amendments					
FY 2008	FY 2009	FY 2010	FY 2011	FY 2012	FY 2013
Target: 80% ≤ 90 days 100% ≤ 2 yrs	85% ≤ 90 days 100% ≤ 2 yrs	90% ≤ 90 days 100% ≤ 2 yrs	90% ≤ 90 days 100% ≤ 2 yrs	92% < 90 days 100% < 2 yrs	92% < 90 days 100% < 2 yrs
Actual: 98% ≤ 90 days 100% ≤ 1 yr	97% ≤ 90 days 100% ≤ 2 yrs	95% ≤ 90 days 100% ≤ 2 yrs	197% < 90 days 100% < 2 years		

Timeliness of Licensing Actions - Review of Applications for Materials License Renewals and Sealed Source and Device Designs.					
FY 2008	FY 2009	FY 2010	FY 2011	FY 2012	FY 2013
Target: 80% ≤ 180 days 100% ≤ 2yrs	80% ≤ 180 days 100% ≤ 2 yrs	90% ≤ 180 days 100% ≤ 2 yrs	92% ≤ 180 days 100% ≤ 2 yrs	92% < 180 days 100% < 2yrs	92% < 180 days 100% < 2yrs
Actual: 94% ≤ 180 days 100% ≤ 2 yrs	91% ≤ 180 days 100% ≤ 2 yrs	95% ≤ 180 days 100% ≤ 2 yrs	97% < 180 days 100% < 2 years		

Oversight

Timeliness of Safety Inspections of Materials Licensees					
FY 2008	FY 2009	FY 2010	FY 2011	FY 2012	FY 2013
Target: >95% completed on time.	>98% completed on time.	>98% completed on time.	>98% completed on time.	>98% completed on time.	>98% completed on time.
Actual: 99% completed on time	99% completed on time.	99% completed on time.	99% completed on time.		

Timeliness in Completing Reviews for Technical Allegations					
FY 2008	FY 2009	FY 2010	FY 2011	FY 2012	FY 2013
Target: 80% ≤ 150 days 90% ≤ 180 days 100% ≤ 360 days	90% ≤ 150 days 95% ≤ 180 days 100% ≤ 360 days	90% ≤ 150 days 95% ≤ 180 days 100% ≤ 360 days	90% ≤ 150 days 95% ≤ 180 days 100% ≤ 360 days	90% ≤ 150 days 95% ≤ 180 days 100% ≤ 360 days	90% ≤ 150 days 95% ≤ 180 days 100% ≤ 360 days
Actual: 92% ≤ 150 days 95% ≤ 180 days 98% ≤ 360 days	98% ≤ 150 days 100% ≤ 180 days 100% ≤ 360 days	94% ≤ 150 days 98% ≤ 180 days 100% ≤ 360 days	95% < 150 days 100% < 180 days 100% < 360 days		

Timeliness in Completing Enforcement Actions

	FY 2008	FY 2009	FY 2010	FY 2011	FY 2012	FY 2013
Target:	Investigation cases: 100% completed within 360 days of OE processing time. Non-Investigation cases: 100% completed within 180 days of OE processing time.	nvestigation cases: 100% completed within 360 days of OE processing time. Non-Investigation cases: 100% completed within 180 days of OE processing time.	Investigation cases: 100% completed within 360 days of OE processing time. Non-Investigation cases: 100% completed within 180 days of OE processing time.	Investigation cases: 100% completed within 360 days of OE processing time. Non-Investigation cases: 100% completed within 180 days of OE processing time.	Investigation cases: 100% completed within 330 days of OE processing time. Non-Investigation cases: 100% completed within 160 days of OE processing	nvestigation cases: 100% completed within 330 days of OE processing time. Non-Investigation cases: 00% completed within 160 days of OE processing time.
Actual:	Investigation: None ≥ 360 days Non-Investigations: None ≥ 180 days	IInvestigation: None ≥ 360 days Non-Investigations: None ≥ 180 days	Investigation: None ≥ 360 days Non-Investigations: None ≥ 180 days	Investigation: None > 360 days Non-Investigation: None > 180 days		

Timeliness in Completing Investigations–Target 1

	FY 2008	FY 2009	FY 2010	FY 2011	FY 2012	FY 2013
Target:	85% of investigations that developed sufficient information to reach a conclusion regarding wrongdoing will be completed in 10 months or less.	85% of investigations that developed sufficient information to reach a conclusion regarding wrongdoing will be completed in 10 months or less.	85% of investigations that developed sufficient information to reach a conclusion regarding wrongdoing will be completed in 9 months or less.s	885% of investigations that developed sufficient information to reach a conclusion regarding wrongdoing will be completed in 9 months or less.	85% of investigations that developed sufficient information to reach a conclusion regarding wrongdoing will be completed in 9 months or less.	85% of investigations that developed sufficient information to reach a conclusion regarding wrongdoing will be completed in 9 months or less.
Actual:	CCompleted 37 investigations in which 100% (37) developed sufficient information to reach a conclusion regarding wrongdoing were completed in 10 months or less.	CCompleted 33 investigations in which 100% (33) reached sufficient information to reach a conclusion regarding wrongdoing were completed in 10 months or less	Completed 18 investigations in which 100% (18) reached sufficient information to reach a conclusion regarding wrongdoing were completed in 9 months or less	Completed 25 investigations in which 88% (22) reached sufficient information to reach a conclusion regarding wrongdoing were completed in 9 months or less		

Timeliness in Completing Investigations–Target 2						
	FY 2008	FY 2009	FY 2010	FY 2011	FY 2012	FY 2013
Target:	Close 100% of OI investigations in time to initiate civil and/or criminal enforcement action.	Close 100% of OI investigations in time to initiate civil and/or criminal enforcement action.	Close 100% of OI investigations in time to initiate civil and/or criminal enforcement action.	Close 100% of OI investigations in time to initiate civil and/or criminal enforcement action.	Close 100% of OI investigations in time to initiate civil and/or criminal enforcement action.	Close 100% of OI investigations in time to initiate civil and/or criminal enforcement action.
Actual:	100%	100%	100%	100%		

Rulemaking

Percentage of Materials and Waste Rulemaking Activities Completed on Schedule						
	FY 2008	FY 2009	FY 2010	FY 2011	FY 2012	FY 2013
Target:	New measure in FY 2009 90%	90%	90%	90%	90%	90%
Actual:		100%	93%	80%		

Research

Acceptable Technical Quality of Agency Research Technical Products						
	FY 2008	FY 2009	FY 2010	FY 2011	FY 2012	FY 2013
Target:	Combined score ≥3.0.	Combined score ≥3.5	Combined score ≥3.5	Combined score ≥3.5.	Combined score > 3.5	Combined score > 3.5
Actual:	4	4	4.6	4.4		

* Critical research programs typically respond to high priority needs from the Commission and NRC's licensing organizations. Critical research programs regarding the highest priority needs identified at the beginning of the fiscal year.

Timeliness of Completing Actions on Critical Research Programs						
	FY 2008	FY 2009	FY 2010	FY 2011	FY 2012	FY 2013
Target:	90% of major milestones met on or before their due date.	90% of major milestones met on or before their due date.	90% of major milestones met on or before their due date.	90% of major milestones met on or before their due date.	90% of major milestones met on or before their due date.	90% of major milestones met on or before their due date.
Actual:	100% across programs.	100% across programs.	100% across programs.	100% across programs.		

The NRC has developed a process to measure the quality of research products using surveys of end-users to determine the usability and value-added of the products. As appropriate, other mechanisms will be developed and added to this process to measure the quality of research products.

Issuance of NRC Import/Export Authorizations

	FY 2008	FY 2009	FY 2010	FY 2011	FY 2012	FY 2013
Target:	Complete reviews for, and issue as appropriate, 150-200 NRC import/export authorizations (NRC licenses or amendments). Staff reviews will be completed for 100% of the cases within 60 days.	Complete reviews for, and issue as appropriate, 150-200 NRC import/export authorizations (NRC licenses or amendments). Staff reviews will be completed for 100% of the cases within 60 days.	Complete reviews for, and issue as appropriate, 150-200 NRC import/export authorizations (NRC licenses or amendments). Staff reviews will be completed for >95% of the cases within 60 days.	Complete reviews for, and issue as appropriate, 150-200 NRC import/export authorizations (NRC licenses or amendments). Staff reviews will be completed for 95% of the cases within 60 days.	Measure discontinued in FY 2012	
Actual:	Completed 136 staff reviews. 95% were completed within 60 days.	Completed 139 staff reviews. 97.8% were completed within 60 days.	Completed 127 staff reviews. 96.1% were completed within 60 days.	Completed 139 staff reviews. 100% were completed within 60 days.		

Spent Fuel Storage and Transportation by Product Line
(Dollars in Millions)

Product Line	FY 2012 Enacted		FY 2013 Request		Delta FY 2013–FY 2012	
	$M	FTE	$M	FTE	$M	FTE
Licensing	12.5	59.1	12.2	58.6	(0.3)	(0.5)
Oversight	4.2	25.7	4.1	25.4	(0.1)	(0.4)
Rulemaking	3.9	12.6	4.8	18.1	0.9	5.5
Research	4.5	20.7	7.0	21.7	2.4	1.0
International Activities	0.9	3.8	0.8	3.8	(0.1)	(0.0)
Generic HLS	0.2	1.0	0.1	1.0	(0.0)	(0.0)
Subtotal	$26.2	122.9	$29.0	128.5	$2.8	5.6
Corporate Support	14.6	32.2	15.6	33.9	1.0	1.7
Total	$40.8	155.1	$44.6	162.4	$3.8	7.3

Numbers may not add due to rounding.

The Spent Fuel Storage and Transportation Business Line activities are conducted to ensure the safe and secure storage of spent fuel to support continued operations and for the safe and secure transport of radioactive materials to support domestic and international commerce. Activities in this business line include Licensing, Oversight, Rulemaking, Research, International Activities, and Generic Homeland Security efforts associated with radioactive material transportation and the storage of spent nuclear fuel.

About three million packages of radioactive materials are shipped each year in the United States by road, rail, air, or water. Regulating the safety of commercial radioactive material shipments is the joint responsibility of the NRC and the Department of Transportation (DOT). The NRC ensures transportation safety by reviewing and certifying shipping package designs for the transport of large quantities of radioactive and fissile materials. In addition, the NRC reviews and certifies shipping package designs for the Department of Energy (DOE). For example, the NRC reviews and certifies packages used to transport transuranic waste to the Waste Isolation Pilot Plant in New Mexico.

Resources in this business line support the following:

> Safety, security, technical, and environmental reviews of spent fuel storage designs, facilities, and transportation packages, including development and update of regulations, standard review plans, and interim staff guidance

> Safety inspections of transportation packages, storage cask vendors, fabricators, Independent Spent Fuel Storage Installation (ISFSI) operations, and security inspections of spent fuel transportation and route surveys

> Resolution of technical issues associated with allowance of burnup credit for transportation packages and spent fuel storage casks, and for the transportation and storage of high-burnup fuels (greater than 45 gigawatt-days/metric ton uranium)

> Evaluation of the adequacy of regulatory programs for ensuring safe and secure storage and transportation of spent nuclear fuel for extended periods beyond the 120-year timeframe currently considered

> Development of a long-term Waste Confidence (WC) rule by including an environmental impact statement (EIS) and updated WC decisions, for the handling and extended storage of spent nuclear fuel for more than 60 years after a reactor's licensed life

> Identification and resolution of regulatory issues associated with extended storage and transportation (EST) of spent nuclear fuel, and initial development of a licensing regulatory framework to accommodate alternative geologic disposal or other disposal options in response to changes in the national program for high-level waste management

> Coordination with domestic and international partners on the safety and security of storage and transport matters

> Legal advice and representation

> Training

The outputs of the product lines under this business line contribute to the scoring of the NRC Safety and Security Performance Measures and their contribution to the achievement of its Strategic Outcomes.

Changes from FY 2012 Enacted Budget

Resources increase within the business line to support the update of the WC rule by FY 2019. This work will also ensure public safety and security by addressing technical and regulatory challenges associated with the extended storage (> 120 years) and subsequent transportation of spent fuel.

Licensing

For FY 2013, the NRC requests $12.2 million, including 58.6 FTE, for licensing activities. This represents a funding decrease of $0.3 million, including 0.5 FTE, when compared with the FY 2012 enacted budget, which does not represent a significant change in workload.

The Licensing Product Line supports safety, security, and environmental licensing activities to confirm licensee requests for radioactive material transportation and interim spent nuclear fuel storage that provides an adequate margin of safety and security consistent with the NRC's rules and regulations. The NRC conducts safety and security reviews of radioactive material transportation package designs; safety and security reviews of spent nuclear fuel storage cask designs and ISFSIs; environmental reviews of ISFSIs; plant-specific security-related licensing reviews, updates to standard review plans, and regulatory infrastructure to ensure licensed activities are conducted in a manner that adequately protects the public health and safety, protects the environment, and promotes the common defense and security.

Licensing resources provide for the following:

> The review of approximately 60 radioactive material transportation package design applications and approximately 20 spent nuclear fuel storage applications to ensure the safe and secure storage of reactor spent fuel

> Technical advice and input into proposed changes in the national strategy for the ultimate disposal of spent nuclear fuel

STRATEGIC GOAL STRATEGIES
SUPPORTED BY LICENSING

Safety—*develop, maintain, and implement licensing and regulatory programs for fuel facilities, materials, spent fuel management, waste management, uranium recovery, and decommissioning activities.*

Security—*use a risk-informed approach to implement appropriate regulatory controls for the possession, handling, import, export, and transshipment of radioactive materials.*

❯ The renewal of the Prairie Island ISFSI license and related environmental assessment support and legal advice and representation on spent fuel storage and radioactive material transportation matters

❯ Transportation certification security reviews, security reviews for onsite storage (licensees under 10 CFR Part 70, "Domestic Licensing of Special Nuclear Material"), issuance of ISFSI security orders, and ISFSI security licensing reviews

❯ Continued development and operation of the Storage Transportation Information Management System and maintenance for the Transportation and Storage Computational Analysis Platform System

❯ The continuation of outreach activities with external stakeholders to demonstrate the safety of the NRC's radioactive material transportation and spent fuel storage regulatory oversight, including support for quarterly meetings of regional transportation groups

Oversight

For FY 2013, the NRC requests $4.1 million, including 25.4 FTE, for oversight activities. This represents a funding decrease of $0.1 million, including 0.4 FTE, when compared with the FY 2012 enacted budget, which does not represent a significant change in workload.

The Oversight Product Line supports the activities of the NRC to continually oversee the safe and secure licensee use of radioactive material transportation packages, spent nuclear fuel storage casks, and ISFSIs; identify significant performance issues; develop generic communications; and ensure licensees take appropriate actions to maintain acceptable operating performance to ensure the adequate protection of public health and safety and the environment.

Oversight resources provide for completion of 16 regional and HQ safety inspections of storage and transportation cask vendors, fabricators, and designers and ISFSI pad construction, dry-run operations, initial loading operations, and routine operations. Resources provide for the identification and implementation of near-term improvements to the storage and transportation inspection, and enforcement programs. Resources also provide for regional security inspection oversight of spent nuclear fuel and wet and dry ISFSI operations. In addition, resources provide for spent nuclear fuel inspection program development, maintenance, update, and route surveys.

Rulemaking

For FY 2013, the NRC requests $4.8 million, including 18.1 FTE, for rulemaking activities. This represents a funding increase of $0.9 million, including 5.5 FTE, when compared with the FY 2012 enacted budget. This increase is to support the update of the WC rule by FY 2019.

The Rulemaking Product Line supports the development and update of rules and regulatory guidance that promote licensee compliance with underlying safety and security principles and requirements. This regulatory framework guides the safety and security activities of the agency and its licensees.

Resources provide for the update of the WC rule by FY 2019 to ensure continued long-term stability of the findings by developing an EIS for long-term storage and handling of spent nuclear fuel. Resources provide for the implementation of a risk-informed regulatory framework for EST of spent nuclear fuel that is enhanced by risk insights and consideration of the integration and harmonization of the NRC's transportation and storage regulations to address EST of spent nuclear fuel. In addition, resources provide for initial development of the analyses and technical bases for rulemaking for alternative disposal strategies, including the evaluation of the interface of other NRC regulations with disposal regulations to ensure safety, security, and environmental protection, and to avoid redundancies and inefficiencies.

Resources also provide for the continuation of efforts on high-priority safety rulemakings related to 10 CFR Part 71 compatibility, Certificates of Compliance (CoCs), and ISFSI Security.

Research

For FY 2013, the NRC requests $7.0 million, including 21.7 FTE, for research activities. This represents a funding increase of $2.4 million, including 1.0 FTE, when compared with the FY 2012 enacted budget. This increase is to support the update of the WC rule by FY 2019.

The Research Product Line supports the NRC's regulatory mission by providing technical advice, tools, and information to identify and resolve safety issues and make regulatory decisions. This includes conducting confirmatory experiments and analyses and preparing the agency for the future through evaluation of the safety aspects of new technologies and designs for radioactive material transportation packages and spent fuel storage casks and ISFSIs; research on technical issues associated with extended and long-term storage; and analysis and modeling for future waste management strategies.

Resources provide for the following:

> Identification of methods, data, and policy issues that are needed to bolster the technical basis for EST and support a WC rule by FY 2019

> Research on technical issues associated with extended dry spent nuclear fuel storage, such as concrete degradation, weld corrosion, impacts of high-burnup and mixed-oxide fuels, climate change impacts on cask performance, transportability of fuel after long-term storage and the need for an improved hazards assessment, including the potential impacts of long-term storage on eventual disposal

> Participation in a U.S. cask demonstration and monitoring program of extended dry cask storage with high-burnup fuel

Resources provide for continued research to obtain and analyze data to support the allowance of full (fission product and actinides) burnup credit for spent boiling water reactor (BWR) fuel transportation and storage casks, evaluate storage and transportation of high-burnup fuels (greater than 45 GWd/MTU), and evaluate the risk of criticality associated with the transportation of spent nuclear fuel.

Resources also provide for analyses, data collection, and modeling for future waste management strategies. Activities include laboratory studies and field investigations to understand key technical issues and risk insights, begin resolution of regulatory gaps, and continued development of the Total-System Performance Assessment tool for risk insights.

STRATEGIC GOAL STRATEGIES
SUPPORTED BY RESEARCH

Safety—improve the NRC's regulatory programs and apply safety-focused research to anticipate and resolve safety issues.

Security—use research to inform the security activities of the agency.

International Activities

For FY 2013, the NRC requests $0.8 million, including 3.8 FTE, for international activities. This represents a funding decrease of $0.1 million, when compared with the FY 2012 enacted budget, which does not represent a significant change in workload.

The International Activities Product Line supports the NRC's international work, which assists decision making, awareness of and responses to emerging technical issues, and promoting best practices in realizing the Safety and Security goals and related strategic measures and outcomes. Additionally, the NRC participates in the development and evaluation of international standards to ensure that they are soundly based and to determine if they should be implemented domestically.

Resources provide for international coordination with the International Atomic Energy Agency (IAEA) to compare regulatory frameworks and share research on storage and transport matters. Resources provide for security activities related to intergovernmental coordination and communication, including coordination with the IAEA and Nuclear Energy Agency in support of safe, secure, and environmentally acceptable transportation and spent fuel storage. Resources also provide for investigation and participation in select international activities, experiments, and collaboration to develop an understanding of the methods used by various countries in dealing with the regulatory, technical, environmental, legal, and programmatic aspects of spent fuel storage and transportation and waste disposal, as well as an understanding of the impact of public and political opinion and the socioeconomic programs developed to address such concerns.

Generic Homeland Security

For FY 2013, the NRC requests $0.1 million, including 1.0 FTE, for generic homeland security activities. There are no significant changes when compared with the FY 2012 enacted budget.

The Generic Homeland Security (HLS) Product Line supports security activities related to intergovernmental coordination and communication. It also supports security activities that are not plant-specific, or associated with a class of licensees, which contribute to the common defense and security of the Nation's critical infrastructure.

Resources provide for ongoing security activities in response to the events of September 11, 2001. This encompasses Generic HLS improvements to address new threats, and it also includes developing interagency agreements and working arrangements with other Federal agencies on issues related to safety, security, and emergency response.

Significant Accomplishments in FY 2011

The NRC completed 57 transportation package design reviews and 11 storage cask and facility license reviews. The review of transportation certification requests and interim storage licensing requests ensures that shipments are made in NRC-approved packages that meet rigorous performance requirements, while supporting the academic, medical, construction, and nuclear power industries that rely on radioisotopes. The review of storage casks and facilities ensures that spent fuel is safely stored, thereby enabling continued reactor and decommissioning activities. The NRC also completed 19 inspections of activities related to radioactive material package certificate holders, spent fuel storage cask certificate holders, and inspections at ISFSIs to ensure that casks are being designed, fabricated, and used according to approved safety requirements.

The NRC published changes to its regulations and associated implementing guidance concerning licensing requirements for the independent storage of spent nuclear fuel, high-level radioactive waste, and reactor-related greater-than-class-C waste. The rule changes extend and clarify the license terms for dry storage cask CoCs and ISFSI licenses. The rule changes also require aging management programs for both specific license and CoC renewals. Finally, the rule changes allow general licensees under 10 CFR Part 72, "Licensing Requirements for the Independent Storage of Spent Nuclear Fuel, High-Level Radioactive Waste, and Reactor- Related Greater Than Class C Waste,"to implement changes authorized by a later CoC amendment to a cask loaded under the initial CoC or an earlier CoC amendment. These rule changes improve the regulatory efficiency of NRC and enhance flexibility of nuclear power utilities in safely managing spent fuel in dry cask storage. The final rule was issued and became effective in FY 2011.

The NRC started research into the safety of extended storage of spent fuel and began a comprehensive review of the spent fuel storage and transportation regulatory programs. This review is evaluating the adequacy of NRC regulatory programs to ensure the safe and secure storage of spent fuel for extended periods beyond 120 years, if needed. It will also include the development of a long-term WC rule, which will systematically evaluate the potential environmental impact of the handling and management of spent nuclear fuel sites for more than 60 years after a reactor's licensed life.

Spent Fuel Storage and Transportation Output Measures

Licensing

Complete Storage Container and Installation Design Reviews Within Timeliness Goals						
	FY 2008	FY 2009*	FY 2010	FY 2011	FY 2012	FY 2013
Target:	80% ≤ 12.6 mos. 100% ≤ 2 yrs.*	80% ≤ 12.6 mos. 100% ≤ 2 yrs.	80% ≤ 12.6 mos. 100% ≤ 2 yrs.	80% ≤ 12.6 mos. 100% ≤ 2 yrs.	80% < 12.6 mos. 100% < 2 yrs.	80% < 12.6 mos. 100% < 2 yrs.
Actual:	90% ≤ 12.6 mos. 100% ≤ 2 yrs.	82% ≤ 12.6 mos. 100% ≤ 2 yrs.	92% ≤ 12.6 mos. 100% ≤ 2 yrs.	100% ≤ 12.6 mos. 100% ≤ 2 yrs.		

Complete Transportation Container Design Reviews Within Timeliness Goals						
	FY 2008	FY 2009*	FY 2010	FY 2011	FY 2012	FY 2013
Target:	80% ≤ 7.4 mos. 100% ≤ 2 yrs.*	80% ≤ 7.4 mos. 100% ≤ 2 yrs.	80% ≤ 7.4 mos. 100% ≤ 2 yrs.	80% ≤ 7.4 mos. 100% ≤ 2 yrs	80% < 7.4 mos. 100% < 2 yrs.	80% < 7.4 mos. 100% < 2 yrs.
Actual:	86% ≤ 7.4 mos. 100% ≤ 2 yrs.	86% ≤ 7.4 mos. 100% ≤ 2 yrs.	87% ≤ 7.4 mos. 100% ≤ 2 yrs.	100% ≤ 7.4 mos. 100% ≤ 2 yrs.		

Utilizing Intra-Agency Contracting						
	FY 2008	FY 2009*	FY 2010	FY 2011	FY 2012	FY 2013
Target:	New measure in FY 2013					Projected savings of $40,000 (50% savings)
Actual:						

Oversight

Number of Spent Fuel Storage and Transportation Inspections Completed						
	FY 2008	FY 2009*	FY 2010	FY 2011	FY 2012	FY 2013
Target:	16 inspections	16 inspections	16 inspections	16 inspections	16 inspections	16 inspections
Actual:	16 inspections	17 inspections	20 inspections	19 inspections		

Timeliness of Completing Actions on Critical Research Programs

	FY 2008	FY 2009*	FY 2010	FY 2011	FY 2012	FY 2013
Target:	90% of major milestones met on or before their due date.	90% of major milestones met on or before their due date.	90% of major milestones met on or before their due date.	90% of major milestones met on or before their due date.	90% of major milestones met on or before their due date.	90% of major milestones met on or before their due date.
Actual:	100% across programs.	100% across programs.	100% across programs.	100% across programs.		

*Critical research programs typically respond to high priority needs from the Commission and NRC's licensing organizations. Critical research programs regarding the highest priority needs identified at the beginning of the fiscal year.

Acceptable Technical Quality of Agency Research Technical Products*

	FY 2008	FY 2009*	FY 2010	FY 2011	FY 2012	FY 2013
Target:	Combined score ≥ 3.0	Combined score ≥ 3.5	Combined score ≥ 3.5	Combined score ≥ 3.5	Combined score ≥ 3.5	Combined score ≥ 3.5
Actual:	4	4	4.6	4.75		

*The NRC has developed a process to measure the quality of research products using surveys of end-users to determine the usability and value-added of the products. As appropriate, other mechanisms will be developed and added to this process to measure the quality of research products.

Waste Confidence and Extended Long-Term Storage Activities - Percent of Planned Products Completed Within a Fiscal Year.

	FY 2008	FY 2009*	FY 2010	FY 2011	FY 2012	FY 2013
Target:	New measure in FY 2013					$\geq 80\%$
Actual:						

DECOMMISSIONING AND LOW-LEVEL WASTE

	FY 2012 Enacted		FY 2013 Request		Delta FY 2013–FY 2012	
Product Line	**$M**	**FTE**	**$M**	**FTE**	**$M**	**FTE**
Licensing	16.4	72.3	17.8	72.8	1.4	0.5
Oversight	4.6	26.3	5.2	27.6	0.7	1.3
Rulemaking	1.2	4.0	0.6	2.2	(0.7)	(1.7)
Research	0.8	5.2	0.4	2.6	(0.4)	(2.6)
International Activities	1.0	5.1	0.9	5.1	(0.0)	(0.0)
Subtotal	$24.0	112.9	$25.0	110.3	$1.0	(2.6)
Corporate Support	13.3	29.3	13.4	29.0	0.1	(0.3)
Total	$37.3	142.1	$38.3	139.3	$1.1	(2.8)

Decommissioning and Low-Level Waste by Product Line (Dollars in Millions)

Numbers may not add due to rounding.

Decommissioning and LLW activities include the licensing and oversight of licensed and unlicensed facilities undergoing decommissioning, the licensing and oversight of new and operating uranium recovery facilities, the oversight of the national LLW management program, and oversight of the DOE waste management activities at the Savannah River and Idaho WIR facilities consistent with the NRC's responsibilities in the Ronald W. Reagan National Defense Authorization Act for FY 2005. This Act requires DOE to consult with the NRC on its WIR determinations for facilities in South Carolina and Idaho as well as NRC monitoring at those sites after waste determinations are completed by DOE. Activities also include interfacing with licensees, applicants, Federal and State agencies, the public, other stakeholders, and Native American Tribal Governments.

Decommissioning is the safe removal of a nuclear facility from service and reduction of residual radioactivity to a level that permits release of the property and termination of the NRC license. The NRC rules for decommissioning establish site-release criteria and provide for unrestricted and, under certain conditions, restricted release of a site. The NRC regulates the decommissioning of complex materials and fuel cycle facilities, power and early test reactors, research and test reactors, and uranium recovery facilities, with the ultimate goal of license termination.

The NRC performs project management, financial, policy, technical, safety, security, and environmental reviews for decommissioning power and early demonstration reactors, research and test reactors, complex materials facilities, and reviews for licensing and operation of uranium recovery facilities. In addition, the NRC develops guidance and import/export reviews of nuclear waste and performs research activities, including the development and improvement of data, models, and other analytical tools for assessing the environmental effects of releases from NRC licensed facilities.

The NRC has organized Decommissioning and LLW activities into product lines that best support Safety and Security strategies and impact strategic outcomes as they relate to decommissioning and LLW activities, uranium recovery licensing, inspection, and related environmental activities. The resources requested support the following five product lines: Licensing, Oversight, Rulemaking, Research, and International Activities.

The outputs of the product lines under this business line contribute to the scoring of the NRC Safety and Security Performance Measures and their contribution to the achievement of its Strategic Outcomes.

Changes from FY 2012 Enacted Budget

Resources increase to better address the uranium recovery licensing actions and environmental reviews as well as the associated legal advice and representation and Licensing Board activities. For the Oversight Product Line, resources increase to perform WIR activities, including monitoring visits at Savannah River and the Idaho National Laboratory sites. For the Rulemaking Product line, resources decrease due to the completion of the Unique Waste Streams rulemaking in early FY 2013.

Licensing

For FY 2013, the NRC requests $17.8 million, including 72.8 FTE, to support licensing activities. This represents a funding increase of $1.4 million, including 0.5 FTE, when compared with the FY 2012 enacted budget. Licensing increases to better address the uranium recovery licensing actions and environmental reviews, as well as the associated legal advice and representation and Licensing Board activities.

The Licensing Product Line supports reviews of requests to terminate a license through a decommissioning process and licensing of uranium recovery and LLW disposal sites. Licensing supports project management, financial, policy, technical, safety, security, and environmental reviews; and other licensing activities supporting operational uranium recovery facilities and the decommissioning power and early demonstration reactors, research and test reactors, complex materials sites, and inactive uranium recovery facilities. Resources support interfaces with NRC licensees, applicants, Federal and State agencies, the public, other stakeholders, and Tribal Governments; in addition to legal advice and representation and Licensing Board activities.

The resources for decommissioning support reviews for 13 power and early demonstration reactors, 9 research and test reactors, 22 decommissioning complex materials facilities, and 38 decommissioning uranium recovery facilities. These activities include reviews of license applications and termination plans, decommissioning plans, reclamation plans, long-term surveillance plans, and license amendments. Complex environmental reviews for decommissioning cases and for licensing actions will also be performed.

The agency will perform safety reviews, environmental reviews, and project management for uranium recovery licensing. FY 2013 resources increase for uranium recovery environmental reviews and will support work on 9 environmental and 10 safety reviews, which include 8 new facilities and 2 operational facilities (hearings included) of applications as well as licensing activities associated with 14 operating uranium recovery facilities. The resources increase for legal advice and representation and Licensing Board activities for activities related to decommissioning power reactors and complex materials sites, uranium recovery licensing, adjudications, and LLW activities.

STRATEGIC GOAL STRATEGIES SUPPORTED BY LICENSING

Safety—oversee the decontamination and decommissioning of nuclear facilities in license termination.

Security—review security plans for decommissioning for consistency with security requirements.

Strategic Goal Strategies Supported by Oversight

Safety—develop, maintain, and implement licensing and regulatory programs for fuel facilities material, spent fuel management, waste management, uranium recovery, and decommissioning.

Security—review security plans and changes for consistency with security requirements.

Strategic Goal Strategies Supported by Rulemaking

Safety—use sound science and state-of-the-art methods to establish, where appropriate, risk-informed and performance-based regulations.

Security—use a risk-informed approach to implement appropriate regulatory controls.

Strategic Goal Strategies Supported by International Activities

Safety—use domestic and international operating experience to inform decision making.

Security—use a risk-informed approach to implement appropriate regulatory controls for the possession, handling, import, export, and transshipment of radioactive materials.

Oversight

For FY 2013, the NRC requests $5.2 million, including 27.6 FTE, to support oversight activities. This represents a funding increase of $0.7 million, including 1.3 FTE, when compared with the FY 2012 enacted budget. Oversight increases to perform WIR activities, including monitoring visits at Savannah River and the Idaho National Laboratory sites.

The Oversight Product Line supports the NRC in continuously overseeing decommissioning and LLW activities to ensure that licensees continue to maintain acceptable safe and secure practices. In FY 2013, resources provide for decommissioning and uranium recovery inspections, LLW program activities, and WIR activities at two DOE sites.

Budgetary resources remain level to perform decommissioning and uranium recovery inspections to ensure that these operations are being conducted safely and in accordance with NRC regulations; and to oversee LLW program activities, which includes updating storage inspection procedures, support of Greater than Class C activities, and support to Agreement States.

Rulemaking

For FY 2013, the NRC requests $0.6 million, including 2.2 FTE, to support rulemaking activities. This represents a funding decrease of $0.7 million, including a decrease of 1.7 FTE, when compared with the FY 2012 enacted budget. This is offset by a decrease due to the Unique Waste Streams rulemaking becoming finalized in early FY 2013 to support WIR activities in Oversight. The Rulemaking Product Line supports the NRC goal of maintaining a safety and security framework of rules, regulatory guidance, and standard review plans that promote licensee compliance with underlying safety principles and security requirements. FY 2013 resources will support work on the regulatory basis for the 10 CFR Part 61 Waste Classification Scheme Rule as well as the guidance development and Environmental Review for the 10 CFR Part 61 Unique Waste Stream Rule.

International Activities

For FY 2013, the NRC requests $0.9 million, including 5.1 FTE, to support international activities. This represents no significant change in funding, when compared with the FY 2012 enacted.

The International Activities Product Line supports activities with international counterparts to exchange information, expertise, operating experiences, and ongoing research to recognize and respond to emerging technical issues and promote best safety and security practices. The NRC also participates in the development of international standards to ensure that they are soundly based and determine whether substantial safety improvements can be identified and incorporated domestically. Resources provide support for international activities and support for bilateral assistance to foreign counterparts on decommissioning issues, licensing of uranium recovery facilities, and development of regulations for the handling and disposal of LLW as well as decommissioning of power reactors and other nuclear facilities.

Resources increase to provide assistance to the IAEA, NEA, IAEA's Waste Safety

Standards Committee, the Joint Convention on the Safety of Spent Fuel Management and on the Safety of Radioactive Waste Management, and many other working groups and committees for the preparation and updating of safety guides and standards. In addition, resources provide for staff assistance to the foreign assignee program and for bilateral and multilateral exchanges of technical information.

Research

For FY 2013, the NRC requests $0.4 million, including 2.6 FTE, to support research activities. This represents a decrease of $0.4 million, including a decrease of 2.6 FTE, when compared with the FY 2012 enacted budget, which does not represent a significant change in workload.

The Research Product Line supports activities to identify, lead, or sponsor reviews that support the resolution of ongoing and future safety issues, including providing tools and expertise needed to support the NRC's independent decisionmaking process. The FY 2013 budget allocates resources to provide analytical assistance on complex licensing cases, such as application of codes for decommissioning reviews and site clean up at sites with uranium contamination and in-situ uranium recovery facilities.

Significant Accomplishments in FY 2011

The agency oversaw decommissioning activities at approximately 85 power and early demonstration reactors, research and test reactors, uranium recovery sites, complex materials sites, and fuel cycle facilities. The agency increased its activities at decommissioning sites containing discrete sources of radium-226 and at Army sites with depleted uranium contamination from military munitions. The agency continued its emphasis on the decommissioning of legacy uranium recovery sites and began several initiatives to improve the program, including updating guidance and enhancing communication with DOE, States, Tribal Governments, and stakeholders.

The NRC conducted regulatory oversight at eight operational uranium recovery sites and reviewed and, if regulations were met, approved the applications for new, restarting, or expanding uranium recovery facilities. The agency had eight applications for new, restarts, or expanding uranium recovery facilities inhouse and the agency worked on seven of those applications. These reviews included both safety and environmental reviews. The agency published the final supplemental environmental impact statements, published the final safety evaluation reports, and granted licenses for the Nichols Ranch and Lost Creek uranium recovery facilities in Wyoming.

The NRC conducted regulatory activities to help ensure the safe management and disposal of low-level radioactive waste generated by radioactive material users, power reactors, and other NRC licensees. The agency performed monitoring visits and issued reports for the DOE's Savannah River Site Saltstone facility. In addition, the agency also conducted outreach with stakeholders and licensees on issues related to issuing guidance on how to classify waste for disposal and potential draft rule language for a proposed change to 10 CFR Part 61 Licensing Requirements for Land Disposal of Radioactive Waste, for site evaluation prior to receiving either long-lived or blended wastes.

STRATEGIC GOAL STRATEGIES SUPPORTED BY RESEARCH

Safety—*improve the NRC's regulatory programs and apply safety-focused research to anticipate and resolve safety issues.*

Security—*use research to inform the security activities of the agency.*

Decommissioning and Low-Level Waste Output Measures

Licensing

	Support Program Licensing Activities by Reviewing Environmental Reports and Preparing Environmental Review Documents					
	FY 2008	FY 2009	FY 2010	FY 2011	FY 2012	FY 2013
Target	Complete 2 final EISs or draft EISs.* Complete 3 complex EAs**.	Complete 1 final EIS or draft EIS.* Complete 3 complex EAs.	Complete 2 draft EIS.* Complete 2 complex EAs.	Complete environmental reviews consistent with the Environmental Protection and Performance Assessment Operating Plan.	Complete environmental reviews consistent with the Environmental Protection and Performance Assessment Operating Plan.	Complete environmental reviews consistent with the Environmental Protection and Performance Assessment Operating Plan.
Actual	Completed the Final EIS for Sequoyah Fuels Corp. and the draft Generic EIS for In-Situ Recovery Uranium Recovery facilities. No complex EAs completed because there were none to complete in FY08.	Completed GEIS for Uranium Recovery. Three complex EAs were completed for Areva, Global Nuclear Fuel - Americas, and Oconee.	Completed draft EISs for AREVA Eagle Rock and GE-Silex license applications. Completed the Final Supplemental EIS for the Moore Ranch ISR license application. Completed one complex EA for the Prairie Island ISFSI License Amendment.	Completed Final Supplemental EISs for the Nichols Ranch and Lost Creek ISR license appplications. Completed Final EIS for AREVA, Eagle Rock Enrichment Facility license application. Issued draft EA (complex) for Nuclear Fuel Service license renewal application for public review and comment. Completed Supplement to the EA (complex) for the Pa'ina Hawaii, LLC Underwater irradiator license application.		

*Within 45 days of acceptance of application and environmental report, publish notice of intent to prepare the EIS and proposed schedule in the Federal Register.

Clean Up Complex Material Sites, Fuel Cycle Sites, Power Reactors, and Research/Test Reactors and Complete Uranium Recovery License Reviews					
FY 2008	FY 2009	FY 2010	FY 2011	FY 2012	FY 2013
Target: Complete decommissioning and uranium recovery licensing actions as scheduled in the Decommissioning Operating Plan. Complete final rule to prevent legacy sites.	Complete decommissioning and uranium recovery licensing actions as scheduled in the Decommissioning Operating Plan.	Complete licensing actions consistent with the Decommissioning Operating Plan.	Complete licensing actions consistent with the Decommissioning Operating Plan.	Complete licensing actions consistent with the Decommissioning Operating Plan.	Complete licensing actions as scheduled in the Decommissioning Operating Plan.
Actual: Completed decommissioning at 8 sites. Completed two uranium recovery licensing actions.	Completed decommissioning at 1 site. Completed final rule for preventing future legacy sites	Consistent with the Decommissioning Operating Plan, completed 15 financial assurance reviews. Completed 55 licensing actions related to decommissioning and operating facilities.	Completed 29 financial assurance reviews. Completed 25 licensing actions related to decommissioning and operating facilities.		

Provide Support to DOE for Waste Incidental to Reprocessing (WIR) Activities

	FY 2008	FY 2009	FY 2010	FY 2011	FY 2012	FY 2013
Target:	Complete monitoring activities as scheduled in the Environmental Protection and Performance Assessment Operating Plan. Complete resolution of 2 WIR generic technical and policy issues identified in FY 2006.	Complete WIR review or monitoring plan/ activities as scheduled in the Environmental Protection and Performance Assessment Operating Plan.	Complete WIR review or monitoring plan/ activities as scheduled in the Environmental Protection and Performance Assessment Operating Plan.	Complete WIR review and monitoring plan activities as scheduled in the Environmental Protection and Performance Assessment Operating Plan.	Complete WIR review and monitoring plan activities as scheduled in the Environmental Protection and Performance Assessment Operating Plan.	Complete WIR review or monitoring plan/ activities as scheduled in the Environmental Protection and Performance Assessment Operating Plan.
Actual:	Completed 4 WIR Monitoring visits and issued 4 WIR Monitoring Reports. Completed resolution of 7 WIR generic technical and policy issues identified in FY 2006.	Completed 3 WIR Monitoring Visits and reviewed 11 Technical Reports related to Saltstone Disposal Facility.	Completed 3 monitoring visits and issued a request for additional information on the revised performance assessment for the Savannah River Site's Saltstone Disposal Facility. Completed 1 monitoring visit for Idaho National Laboratory.	Completed 2 monitoring visits and issued a second request for additional information for the Savannah River Site's Saltstone Disposal Facility. Issued a request for additional information and technical evaluation report for the Savannah River Site's F Tank Farm. Issued a request for additional information, a waste determination, and technical evaluation report for the West Valley melter.		

Timeliness of Completing Actions on Critical Research Programs*					
	FY 2008	FY 2009	FY 2010	FY 2011	FY 2012	FY 2013
Target:	90% of major milestones met on or before their due date.	90% of major milestones met on or before their due date.	90% of major milestones met on or before their due date.	90% of major milestones met on or before their due date.	90% of major milestones met on or before their due date.	90% of major milestones met on or before their due date.
Actual:	100% across programs.	100% across programs.	100% across programs.			

*Critical research programs typically respond to high-priority needs from the Commission and NRC's licensing organizations. Critical research programs regarding the highest priority needs were identified at the beginning of the FY.

Acceptable Technical Quality of Agency Research Technical Products*					
	FY 2008	FY 2009	FY 2010	FY 2011	FY 2012	FY 2013
Target:	Combined score ≥3.0*	Combined score ≥3.5	Combined score ≥3.5	Combined score ≥3.5	Combined score ≥3.5	Combined score ≥ 3.5
Actual:	4	4	4.6	N/A**		

*The NRC has developed a process to measure the quality of research products using surveys of endusers to determine the usability and value-added of the products. As appropriate, other mechanisms will be developed and added to this process to measure the quality of research products.
**No research products produced for this Business Line during FY 2011.

Acceptable Technical Quality of Agency Research Technical Products*					
	FY 2008	FY 2009	FY 2010	FY 2011	FY 2012	FY 2013
Target:	Combined score ≥3.0*	Combined score ≥3.5	Combined score ≥3.5	Combined score ≥3.5	Combined score ≥3.5	Combined score ≥ 3.5
Actual:	4	4	4.6	N/A**		

*The NRC has developed a process to measure the quality of research products using surveys of endusers to determine the usability and value-added of the products. As appropriate, other mechanisms will be developed and added to this process to measure the quality of research products.
**No research products produced for this Business Line during FY 2011.

International Activities

Provide Support to IAEA Waste Safety Standards Committee Reviews, Consultancies/Expert Missions, Joint Convention and Nuclear Energy Agency Support					
	FY 2008	FY 2009	FY 2010	FY 2011	FY 2012	FY 2013
Target:	New measure in FY 2012				Complete actions as scheduled in the Decommissioning and Environmental Protection and Performance Assessment Operating Plans.	Complete actions as scheduled in the Decommissioning and Environmental Protection and Performance Assessment Operating Plans.
Actual:						

Efficiency

Eliminate the Need for Some Site Specific Environmental Impact Statements (I.E. by Reducing Resource Needs) by Developing a Generic Environmental Impact Statement (GEIS) for Uranium Recovery Environmental Reviews*					
	FY 2008	FY 2009	FY 2010	FY 2011	FY 2012	FY 2013
Target:	New measure in FY 2009	Projected savings of $1,040K and 1 FTE	Projected Savings of $1,100K and 4 FTE	Projected savings of $450K and 0.7 FTE	Projected savings of $450K and 0.7 FTE	Projected savings of $450K and 0.7 FTE
Actual:		$2.2 million and 0.6 FTE	$1.2 million and 0 FTE**	$773 thousand and 0 FTE**		

*Between FY 2008 and FY 2013, the staff expects to receive 18 in-situ recovery (ISR) uranium recovery license applications. The development of a Generic Environmental Impact Statement (GEIS) is expected to eliminate the need to develop site-specific environmental impact statements (EISs) for some of these applications. Rather than developing a site-specific EIS for each site the staff will be able to "tier off" the GEIS and instead rely on a less resource- intensive supplemental environmental impact statement or a site specific supplemental EIS to evaluate the environmental impacts of the site-specific ISR license request (total savings of at least $2.0M and 7.0 FTE in FY 2008-FY 2011 and beyond). The final GEIS was issued in June 2009 on schedule.

**Target not met due to a decrease in actual number of reviews and increasing stakeholder involvement.

PERFORMANCE MEASUREMENT

PERFORMANCE MEASUREMENT

The NRC's Strategic Plan for FY 2008–2013 describes the agency's mission and establishes the Commission's direction by defining its goals, strategic outcomes, and strategies and means. The plan's goal structure ensures a focus on outcomes. The FY 2013 Performance Budget uses the Strategic Plan structure to align resources and to show a clear linkage between programs and the agency's goals.

Measuring and monitoring performance is one of the four components of the NRC's Planning, Budgeting, and Performance Management (PBPM) process. The other components are: Setting the Strategic Direction, Determining Planned Activities and Resources, Measuring and Monitoring Performance, and Assessing Performance.

The components of the PBPM process are closely linked and complementary, reflecting a continuous cycle of performance management centered on outcomes. This document integrates the agency's PBPM functions by aligning resources with the agency's goals and establishing performance measures to enable periodic measurement and monitoring of program execution. Annual performance assessments are used to analyze performance and seek improvements in effectiveness and efficiency.

U.S. NUCLEAR REGULATORY COMMISSION STRATEGIC GOALS

Safety—*ensure adequate protection of public health and safety and the environment.*

Security—*ensure adequate protection in the secure use and management of radioactive materials.*

RELATING GOALS TO RESOURCES

The NRC has implemented the PBPM process to accomplish performance budgeting, performance measuring and monitoring, and performance assessments within the agency.

The performance budget integrates the agency's PBPM functions by aligning resources with the agency's goals and establishing performance measures to enable measurement and monitoring of program execution. The business line descriptions in this document identify how each business line contributes to the strategic goals of Safety or Security.

The agency has aligned its budget and accounting structures. This enables the NRC to use cost and other financial data together to evaluate agency program performance. The integration of financial, budget, and performance data provides managers the kind of information that can be used to drive improved agency performance.

The NRC identifies which activities under the agency's two major program areas support the NRC's outcome-based performance measures and uses these as guides to formulate the budget. Specifically, the agency develops program considerations and priorities, which identify key external factors and internal influences that would significantly affect the NRC's work activities and resource requirements. For each major activity, the NRC identifies the products needed to achieve the outcome-based performance measures, taking into consideration the program considerations and priorities. The NRC also identifies and prioritizes products needed based on their contribution to goals. Lastly, the NRC

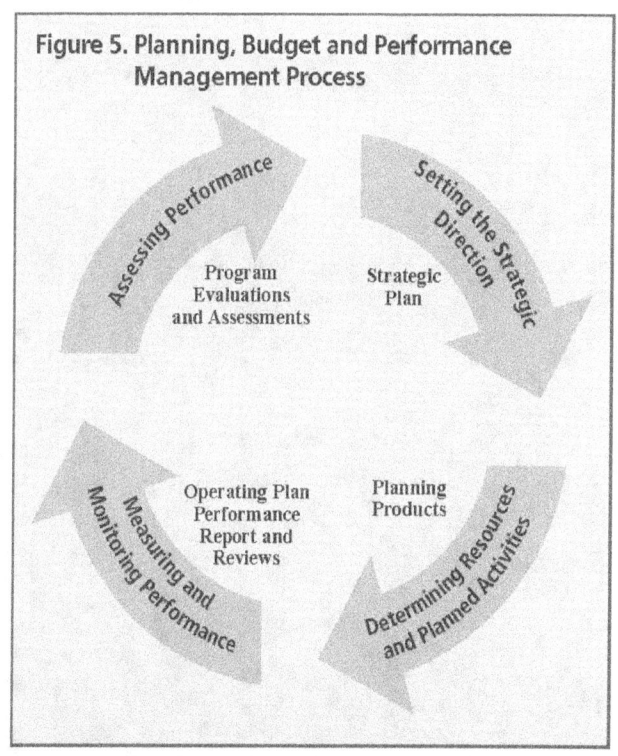

Figure 5. Planning, Budget and Performance Management Process

Assessing Performance

Setting the Strategic Direction

Program Evaluations and Assessments

Strategic Plan

Operating Plan Performance Report and Reviews

Planning Products

Measuring and Monitoring Performance

Determining Resources and Planned Activities

determines the resource requirements needed to achieve each product, forming the basis for developing the agency's budget for each program area. Each of NRC's performance budget review levels takes into consideration those factors described above in relating outcome-based and output-based performance measures to resources in making budget recommendations and decisions.

Goals

The table below shows the alignment of the NRC fully costed Nuclear Reactor Safety Program and Nuclear Materials and Waste Safety Program with the Safety and Security goals. The full cost includes an allocation of the agency's infrastructure and support costs to specific programs.

Alignment of Resources to NRC Goals (Dollars in Millions) (Excludes OIG)						
	FY 2012 Enacted			FY 2013 Request		
Major Programs	Safety	Security	Total	Safety	Security	Total
Nuclear Reactor Safety	757.2	42.1	799.3	767.6	43.5	809.7
Nuclear Materials and Waste Safety	213.1	30.9	243.9	198.4	32.7	232.5
Total	$948.8	$78.5	$1,027.2	$966	$76.2	$1,042.2

Numbers may not add due to rounding.

PERFORMANCE MEASURES

Goal: Safety

Number of New Conditions Evaluated as Red by the NRC's Reactor Oversight Process[*]

	FY 2008	FY 2009	FY 2010	FY 2011	FY 2012	FY 2013
Target:	≤3	≤3	≤3	≤3	≤3	≤3
Actual:	0	0	0	1		

[*] This measure is the number of new red inspection findings during the FY, plus the number of new red performance indicators during the fiscal year. Programmatic issues at multiunit sites that result in red findings for each individual unit are considered separate conditions for purposes of reporting for this measure. A red performance indicator and a red inspection finding that are due to an issue with the same underlying causes are also considered separate conditions for purposes of reporting for this measure. Red inspection findings are included in the FY in which the final significance determination was made. Red performance indicators are included in the FY in which ROP external Web page was updated to show the red indicator.

Number of Significant Accident Sequence Precursors of a Nuclear Reactor Accident[*]

	FY 2008	FY 2009	FY 2010	FY 2011	FY 2012	FY 2013
Target:	≤ 0	≤ 0	≤ 0	≤ 0	≤ 0	≤ 0
Actual:	0	0	0	0		

[*] Significant accident sequence precursor (ASP) events have a conditional core damage probability (CCDP) or ΔCDP of > 1x 10-3. Such events have a 1/1000 (10-3) or greater probability of leading to a reactor accident involving core damage. An identical condition affecting more than one plant is counted as a single ASP event if a single accident initiator would have resulted in a single reactor accident.

Number of Operating Reactors Whose Integrated Performance Entered the Manual Chapter 0350 Process, the Multiple/Repetitive Degraded or Unacceptable Cornerstone of the Reactor Oversight Program (ROP) Action Matrix With No Performance Exceeding Abnormal Occurrence Criterion I.D.4.[*]

	FY 2008	FY 2009	FY 2010	FY 2011	FY 2012	FY 2013
Target:	≤ 3	≤ 3	≤ 3	≤ 3	TBD	≤ 3
Actual:	0	0	0	2		

[*] This measure is the number of plants that have entered the Manual Chapter 0350 process, the multiple/repetitive degraded cornerstone column, or the unacceptable performance column during the FY (i.e., were not in these columns or process the previous FY). Data for this measure are obtained from the NRC external Web Action Matrix Summary page, which provides a matrix of the five columns with the plants listed within their applicable column and notes the plants in the Manual Chapter 0350 process. For reporting purposes, plants that are the subject of an approved deviation from the Action Matrix are included in the column or process in which they appear on the Web page. The target value is set based on the expected addition of several indicators and a change in the long-term trending methodology (which will no longer be influenced by the earlier data and will be more sensitive to changes in current performance).

PERFORMANCE MEASUREMENT

Number of Significant Adverse Trends in Industry Safety Performance With No Trend Exceeding the Abnormal Occurance Criterion I.D.4*

	FY 2008	FY 2009	FY 2010	FY 2011	FY 2012	FY 2013
Target:	≤ 1	≤ 1	≤ 1	≤ 1	≤ 1	≤ 1
Actual:	0	0	0	0		

*Considering all indicators qualified for use in reporting.

Number of Events With Radiation Exposures to the Public and Occupational Workers that Exceed Abnormal Occurrence Criterion I.A.3*

	FY 2008	FY 2009	FY 2010	FY 2011	FY 2012	FY 2013
Reactor Target:	0	0	0	0	0	0
Actual:	0	0	0	0		
Material Target:	≤ 2	≤ 2	≤ 2	≤ 2	≤ 2	≤ 2
Actual:	0	0	0	0		
Waste Target:	0	0	0	0	0	0
Actual:	0	0	0	0		

* Releases for which a 30-day report requirement is required under 10 CFR 20.2203(a)(3).

Number of Radiological Releases to the Environment that Exceed Applicable Regulatory Limits*

	FY 2008	FY 2009	FY 2010	FY 2011	FY 2012	FY 2013
Reactor Target:[6]	0	0	0	0	0	0
Actual:	0	0	0	0		
Material Target:	≤ 2	≤ 2	≤ 2	≤ 2	≤ 2	≤ 2
Actual:	0	0	0	0		
Waste Target:	0	0	0	0	0	0
Actual:	0	0	0	0		

*With no event exceeding AO Criterion 1.B.1.
** Releases for which a 30-day report is requirement under 10 CFR 20.2203(a)(3).

PERFORMANCE MEASURES

Goal: Security

Unrecovered Losses or Thefts of Risk-Significant* Radioactive Sources

	FY 2008	FY 2009	FY 2010	FY 2011	FY 2012	FY 2013
Target:	0	0	0	0	0	0
Actual:	0	0	0	1**		

*"Risk-significant" is defined as any unrecovered lost or abandoned sources, that exceed the values listed in Appendix P to 10 CFR Part 110 - High Risk Radioactive Material, Category 2. Excluded from reporting under this criterion are those events involving sources that are lost or abandoned under the following conditions: (1) sources abandoned in accordance with the requirements of 10 CFR 39.77(c) (2), (2) recovered sources with sufficient indication that doses in excess of the reporting thresholds specified in Abnormal Occurrence (AO) Criteria I.A.1 and I.A.2 did not occur during the time the source was missing, (3) unrecoverable sources lost under such conditions that doses in excess of the reporting thresholds specified in AO Criteria I.A.1 and I.A.2 were not known to have occurred, (4) other sources that are lost or abandoned and declared unrecoverable, (5) for which the agency has made a determination that the risk-significance of the source is low based upon the locations (e.g., water depth) or physical characteristics (e.g., half-life, housing) of the source and its surroundings, (6) where all reasonable efforts have been made to recover the source, and (7) it has been determined that the source is not recoverable and will not be considered a realistic safety or security risk under this measure.

**There were no losses and one theft of radioactive nuclear material that the NRC considered to be risk significant during FY 2011. The agency will coordinate and review the increased controls applied to these sources and determine if additional controls need to be implemented for these sources.

Number of Substantiated* Cases of Actual Theft or Diversion of Licensed, Risk-Significant Radioactive Sources or Formula Quantities** of Special Nuclear Material; or Attacks that Result in Radiological Sabotage***

	FY 2008	FY 2009	FY 2010	FY 2011	FY 2012	FY 2013
Target:	0	0	0	0	0	0
Actual:	0	0	0	0		

*"Substantiated" means a situation in which an indication of loss, theft, or unlawful diversion, such as an allegation of diversion, report of lost or stolen material, statistical processing difference, or other indication of loss of material control or accountability, cannot be refuted following an investigation and requires further action on the part of the agency or other proper authorities.

**A formula quantity of special nuclear material is defined in 10 CFR 70.4.

***"Radiological sabotage" is defined in 10 CFR 73.2.

Number of Substantiated* Losses of Formula Quantities of Special Nuclear Material or Substantiated Inventory Discrepancies of Formula Quantities of Special Nuclear Material that are Judged to be Caused by Theft or Diversion or by Substantial Breakdown of the Accountability System.

	FY 2008	FY 2009	FY 2010	FY 2011	FY 2012	FY 2013
Target:	0	0	0	0	0	0
Actual:	0	0	0	0		

* "Substantiated" means a situation which an indication of loss, theft, or unlawful diversion such as an allegation of diversion, report of lost or stolen material, statistical processing difference, or other indication of loss of material control or accountability, cannot be refuted following an investigation and requires further action on the part of the agency or other proper authorities.

PERFORMANCE MEASUREMENT

Number of Substantial Breakdowns* of Physical Security or Material Control (I.E., Access Control, Containment, or Accountability Systems) that Significantly Weakened the Protection against Theft, Diversion, or Sabotage.

	FY 2008	FY 2009	FY 2010	FY 2011	FY 2012	FY 2013
Target:	≤ 1	≤ 1	≤ 1	≤ 1	≤ 1	≤ 1
Actual:	0	0	0	0		

*A "substantial breakdown" is defined as a red finding in the security cornerstone of the ROP, or any plant or facility determined to either have overall unacceptable performance or be in a shutdown condition (inimical to the effective functioning of the Nation's critical infrastructure) as a result of significant performance problems or operational events.

Number of Significant Unauthorized Disclosures of Classified and/or Safeguards Information.*

	FY 2008	FY 2009	FY 2010	FY 2011	FY 2012	FY 2013
Target:	0	0	0	0	0	0
Actual:	0	0	0	0		

*"Significant unauthorized disclosure" is defined as a disclosure that harms national security or public health or safety.

DATA COLLECTION PROCEDURES FOR VERIFICATION AND VALIDATION OF PERFORMANCE MEASURES

Most of the data used to measure the NRC's performance against its strategic goals related to safety and security are obtained or derived from the NRC's AO data and reports or preliminary notifications of events submitted by licensees. The AO criteria have been amended to ensure that they are consistent with the NRC's Strategic Plan for FY 2008–2013 and the NRC rulemaking on Title 10 of the Code of Federal Regulations (10 CFR) Part 35.

The NRC developed its AO criteria to comply with the legislative intent of Section 208 of the Energy Reorganization Act of 1974, as amended. The Act requires the NRC to inform Congress of unscheduled incidents or events that the Commission determines to be significant from the standpoint of public health and safety. Events that meet the AO criteria are included in an annual "Report to Congress on Abnormal Occurrences" (NUREG-0090). In addition, in 1997, the Commission determined that events occurring at Agreement State licensed facilities that meet the AO criteria should be reported in the annual AO report to Congress. Therefore, the AO criteria developed by the NRC are uniformly applied to events that occur at facilities licensed or otherwise regulated by the NRC and the Agreement States.

Data for AOs originate from external sources, such as Agreement States and NRC licensees. The NRC believes these data are credible because (1) the information needed from external sources is required to be reported to the NRC by regulations, (2) the NRC maintains an aggressive inspection program that, among other activities, audits licensees and evaluates Agreement State programs to determine whether information is being reported as required by the regulations, and (3) there are agency procedures for reviewing and evaluating licensees. The NRC database systems for safety that support this process include the Licensee Event Report Search System (LER Search), the ASP database, the Nuclear Material Events Database (NMED), and the Radiation Exposure Information Report System. The NRC database systems for security that support this process include Suspicious Incidents Data System (SIDS).

The NRC has established procedures for the systematic review and evaluation of events reported by NRC licensees and Agreement State licensees. The objective of the review is to identify events that are significant from the standpoint of public health and safety based on criteria that include specific thresholds. The NRC uses a number of sources to determine the reliability and the technical accuracy of event information reported to the NRC. Such sources include (1) NRC licensee reports, (2) NRC inspection reports, (3) Agreement State reports, (4) periodic review of Agreement State regulatory programs, (5) NRC consultant/contractor reports, and (6) U.S. Department of Energy Operating Experience Weekly Summaries. In addition, there are daily interactions and exchanges of event information between Headquarters (HQ) and the regional offices, as well as periodic conference calls among HQ, the regions, and Agreement States to discuss event information. Identified events that meet the AO criteria are validated and verified by all applicable NRC HQ program offices, regional offices, and agency management before submission to Congress.

The following performance measures have been identified for verification and validation.

Goal 1—Safety: Ensure adequate protection of public health and safety and the environment.

Nuclear Reactor Safety

Strategic Outcomes:

Prevent the occurrence of any nuclear reactor accidents.

Prevent the occurrence of any inadvertent criticality events.

Prevent the occurrence of any acute radiation exposures resulting in fatalities.

Prevent the occurrence of any releases of radioactive materials that result in significant radiation exposures.

Prevent the occurrence of any releases of radioactive materials that cause significant adverse environmental impacts.

Performance Measures:

1—Number of new conditions evaluated as red by the NRC's reactor oversight process.

Reactor Safety Target: Less than or equal to three

Verification: The data for this performance measure are collected in two ways as part of the NRC's ROP. Inspection findings are collected at least quarterly by NRC inspectors. Inspectors use formal detailed inspection procedures to review plant operations and maintenance. Inspection findings are reviewed by NRC managers to assess their significance as part of the ROP's significance determination process (SDP). The data for performance indicators are collected by licensees and submitted to the NRC at least quarterly. The significance of the data is determined by thresholds for each indicator. The NRC conducts inspections of licensee processes for collecting and submitting the data to ensure completeness, accuracy, consistency, timeliness, and validity.

The NRC enhances the quality of its inspections through inspector feedback and periodic reviews of results. The inspectors are trained through a rigorous qualification program. The quality of performance indicators is improved through continuous feedback from licensees and inspectors that is incorporated into guidance documents. The NRC publishes the inspection findings and performance indicators on the agency's Web site, and incorporates feedback received from all stakeholders as appropriate.

Validation: The inspection findings and performance indicators used by the ROP cover a broad range of plant operations and maintenance. NRC managers review significant issues that are identified and inspectors conduct supplemental inspections of selected aspects of plant operations as appropriate. Plants that are identified as having performance issues, as well as a self-assessment of the ROP, are reviewed by senior agency managers on an annual basis, and the results are reported to the Commission.

This measure is the number of new red inspection findings plus the number of new red performance indicators during the FY. Programmatic issues at multiunit sites that result in red findings for each individual unit are considered separate conditions for purposes of reporting for this measure. A red performance indicator and a red inspection finding that are due to an issue with the same underlying causes are also considered separate conditions for purposes of reporting for this measure. Red inspection findings are included in the FY in which the final significance determination was made. Red performance indicators are included in the FY in which the ROP external Web page was updated to show the red indicator.

2–Number of significant accident sequence precursors of a nuclear accident.

Reactor Safety Target: Zero

Verification: The NRC has an ASP program to evaluate U.S. nuclear power plant operating experience systematically to identify, document, and rank those operating events that were most significant in terms of the potential for inadequate core cooling and core damage (i.e., precursors). The ASP program evaluation process has five steps. First, the NRC screens operating experience data to identify events and/or conditions that may be potential precursors to a nuclear accident. The data that are evaluated include LERs from the LER Search database; Incident Investigation Team or Augmented Inspection Team reviews the NRC's daily screening of operational events and other events identified by NRC staff as candidates. The second step is to conduct an engineering review of these screened events, using specific criteria, to identify those events requiring detailed analyses as candidate precursors. Third, the NRC staff calculates a CCDP by mapping failures observed during the event to accident sequences in risk models. Fourth, the preliminary potential precursor analyses are provided to the NRC staff and the licensee for independent peer review. However, for ASP analyses of noncontroversial, low-risk precursors in which the ASP results reasonably agree with the SDP results, formal peer reviews by licensees may not be performed. The NRC staff will continue to perform an in-house review process for all analyses. Lastly, findings from the analyses are provided to the licensee and the public.

It must also be noted that there is a time lag in obtaining ASP analysis results, since they are often based on LERs (submitted up to 60 days after an event) and most analyses take approximately 6 months to complete. Final data will be reported in the year in which the event occurred.

Validation: The ASP program identifies significant precursors as those events that have a 1/1000 (10^{-3}) or greater probability of leading to a nuclear reactor accident. Significant accident sequence precursor events have a CCDP or ΔCDP of $> 1 \times 10^{-3}$.

3–Number of operating reactors whose integrated performance entered the Manual Chapter 0350 process, the multiple/repetitive degraded cornerstone column, or the unacceptable performance column of the ROP Action Matrix with no performance exceeding Abnormal Occurrence Criterion I.D.4.

Reactor Safety Target: Less than or equal to three

Verification: The data for this performance measure are collected by the NRC ROP on a continuous basis, and the information is published at least quarterly. NRC inspectors use detailed formal procedures to conduct inspections of licensee performance, and NRC managers review the results to ensure the completeness, accuracy, consistency, timeliness, and validity of the data.

The NRC enhances the quality of its inspections through inspector feedback and periodic reviews of results. The inspectors are trained through a rigorous qualification program. The quality is also improved through continuous feedback from licensees and inspectors that is incorporated into guidance documents. The NRC publishes the data on the agency's Web site and incorporates feedback received from all stakeholders as appropriate.

Validation: The information collected by the ROP covers a broad range of plant operations and maintenance. NRC managers review significant issues that are identified and inspectors conduct supplemental inspections of selected aspects of plant operations as appropriate. Plants that are identified as having performance issues are reviewed by senior agency managers on an annual basis, and the results are reported to the Commission. The same is true of the agency's self-assessment of the ROP.

This measure is the number of plants that have entered the Manual Chapter 0350 process, the multiple/repetitive degraded cornerstone column, or the unacceptable performance column during the FY (i.e., were not in these columns or process the previous FY). Data for this measure are obtained from the NRC external Web Action Matrix Summary page that provides a matrix of the five columns with the plants listed within their applicable column and notes the plants in the Manual Chapter 0350 process. For reporting purposes, plants that are the subject of an approved deviation from the Action Matrix are included in the column or process in which they appear on the Web page.

4–Number of significant adverse trends in industry safety performance with no trend exceeding the Abnormal Occurrence Criterion I.D.4.

Reactor Safety Target: Less than or equal to one

Verification: The data for this performance measure are derived from data supplied by all power plant licensees in LERs and from monthly operating reports, as well as performance indicator data submitted for the ROP. These data are required by 10 CFR 50.73, Licensee Event report System and/or plant-specific technical specifications, or are submitted by all plants as part of the ROP. Detailed NRC guidelines and procedures are in place to control each of these reporting processes. The NRC reviews these procedures for appropriateness both periodically and in response to licensee feedback. The NRC also conducts periodic inspections of licensees' processes for collecting and submitting the data to ensure completeness, accuracy, consistency, timeliness, and validity.

All licensees report the data at least quarterly. The NRC staff reviews all of the data and conducts inspections to verify safety-significant information. The NRC also employs a contractor to review the data submitted by licensees, input the data into a database, and compile the data into various indicators. Quality assurance processes for this work have been established and included in the statement of work for the contract. The experience and training of key personnel are controlled through administration of the contract. The contractor identifies discrepancies to both licensees and the NRC for resolution. The NRC reviews the indicators and publishes them on the agency's Web site on a quarterly basis. The agency also incorporates feedback from licensees and the public, where appropriate.

The target value is set based on the expected addition of several indicators and a change in the long-term trending methodology.

Validation: The data and indicators that support reporting against this performance measure provide a broad range of information on nuclear power plant performance. The NRC staff tracks indicators and applies statistical techniques to provide an indication of whether industry performance is improving, steady, or degrading over time. If the staff identifies any adverse trends, the NRC addresses the problem through its processes for addressing generic safety issues and issuing generic communications to licensees. The NRC is developing additional, risk-informed indicators to enhance the current set of indicators. In doing so, the staff considers the costs and benefits of collecting the data through ongoing, extensive interactions with industry regarding the indicators. The Industry Trends Program is reviewed by senior agency managers on an annual basis, and the results are reported to the Commission.

5–Number of events with radiation exposures to the public and occupational workers from nuclear reactors that exceed Abnormal Occurrence Criterion I.A.3

Reactor Safety Target: Zero

Verification: Licensees report overexposures through the LER process, which are then entered into a searchable database. The database is used to identify those LERs that report overexposures. NRC resident inspectors stationed at each nuclear power plant provide a high degree of assurance that all events meeting reporting criteria are reported to the NRC. In addition, the NRC conducts inspections if there is any indication that an exposure exceeded, or could have exceeded, a regulatory limit. Finally, areas of the facility that may be subject to radiation contamination have monitors that record radiation levels. These monitors would immediately reveal any instances in which high levels of radiation exposure occurred.

Validation: Given the nature of the process of using radioactive materials to generate power, overexposure to radiation is a potential danger from the operation of nuclear power plants. Such exposure to radiation in excess of the applicable regulatory limits may potentially occur through either a nuclear accident or other malfunctions at the plant. Consequently, tracking the number of overexposures that occur at nuclear reactors is an important indicator of the degree to which safety is being maintained.

6-Number of radiological releases to the environment from nuclear
reactors that exceed applicable regulatory limits.

Reactor Safety Target: Zero

Verification: As with worker overexposures, licensees report environmental releases
of radioactive materials that are in excess of regulations or license conditions through
the LER process, which are then entered into a searchable database. The database is
used to identify those LERs reporting releases and the number of reported releases is
then applied to this measure. The NRC also conducts periodic inspections of licensees
to ensure that they properly monitor and control releases to the environment through
effluent pathways. In addition, onsite monitors would record any instances in which the
plant releases radiation into the environment. If the inspections or the monitors reveal
any indication that an accident or inadvertent release has occurred, the NRC conducts
followup inspections.

Validation: The generation of nuclear power creates radioactive materials that are
released into the environment in a controlled manner. These radioactive discharges are
subject to regulatory controls that limit the amount discharged and the resultant dose
to members of the public. Consequently, the NRC tracks all releases of radioactive
materials in excess of regulatory limits as a performance measure because large
releases in excess of regulatory limits have the potential to endanger public safety or
harm the environment. The NRC inspects every nuclear power plant for compliance
with regulatory requirements and specific license conditions related to radiological
effluent releases. The inspection program includes enforcement actions to be taken for
violations of the regulations or license conditions, based on the severity of the event.

This performance measure includes dose values that are classified as being as low as
reasonably achievable (ALARA), contained in Appendix I to 10 CFR Part 50 as well as
the public dose limits contained in 10 CFR Part 20: Because the performance measure
includes ALARA values, which are not safety limits, and because Appendix I to 10
CFR Part 50 allows licensees to temporarily exceed the ALARA dose values, for good
reason, the performance measure is set to two.

Nuclear Material and Waste Safety

Strategic Outcomes:

Prevent the occurrence of any inadvertent criticality events.

Prevent the occurrence of any acute radiation exposures resulting in fatalities.

Prevent the occurrence of any releases of radioactive materials that result in significant
radiation exposures.

Prevent the occurrence of any releases of radioactive materials that cause significant
adverse environmental impacts.

Performance Measures:

Materials Safety Target: Less than or equal to two

Waste Safety Target: Zero

Verification: This performance measure includes any event involving licensed radioactive materials that results in significant radiation exposures to members of the public and/or occupational workers that exceed the dose limits in the AO reporting criteria. Due to the extremely high doses employed during medical applications of radioactive materials, it is also appropriate to use a radiation exposure that results in unintended permanent functional damage to an organ or a physiological system, as determined by a physician, as a criterion for this measure. AO Criterion I.A is used as the basis for this measure.

Should an event meeting this threshold occur, it would be reported to the NRC and/or Agreement States through a number of sources, but primarily through required licensee notifications. These events are summarized in event notifications and preliminary notifications, which are used to widely disseminate the information to internal and external stakeholders.

The fuel facilities, nuclear material users, spent fuel storage and transportation, decommissioning, and low-level waste, and high-level waste repository programs contain elements that verify the completeness and accuracy of licensee reports. The Integrated Materials Performance Evaluation Program (IMPEP) also provides a mechanism to verify that Agreement States and NRC regions are consistently collecting and reporting such events as received from the licensees and entering them into NMED.

The NRC has taken a number of steps to improve the timeliness and completeness of materials event data. These steps include assessment of the NMED data during monthly staff reviews; emphasis and analysis during the IMPEP reviews; NMED training in HQ, the regions, and in Agreement States; and discussions at all Agreement State and the Conference of Radiation Control Program Directors (CRCPD) meetings.

Validation: There is a logical basis for using events involving radiation exposures to the public and occupational workers from radioactive material that exceed AO Criterion I.A., as a performance measure for ensuring the protection of public health and safety. An event is considered an AO if it is determined to be significant from the standpoint of public health or safety. The NRC's regulatory process, including licensing, inspection, guidance, regulations, and enforcement activities, is designed to mitigate the likelihood of an event that would exceed AO Criterion I.A.

Events of this magnitude are rare. In the unlikely event that an AO should occur, the NRC or Agreement State technical specialists will confirm whether the criteria were met, with input provided by expert consultants, as necessary.

The NRC does not use statistical sampling of data to determine results. Rather, all event data are reviewed to determine if the performance measure has been met. There are two important data limitations in determining this performance measure. These include delay time for receiving information and/or the failure of the NRC to become aware of an event that causes significant radiation exposures to the public or occupational workers. The NRC regulations associated with event reporting include specific requirements for timely notifications; there is a lag time separating the occurrence of an event and the known consequences of an event.

The NRC believes the probability of not being aware of an event that causes significant radiation exposures to the public or occupational workers is very small. Periodic licensee inspections and regulatory reporting requirements are sufficient to ensure that an event of this magnitude would become known. If such an event occurred, it would result in a prompt and thorough investigation of the event, its consequences, its root causes, and the necessary actions by the licensee and the NRC to mitigate the situation and prevent recurrence. In addition to these immediate actions, the NRC holds periodic meetings, where staff and management validate the occurrence of these events.

2–Number of radiological releases to the environment that exceed applicable regulatory limits.

Materials Safety Target: Less than or equal to two

Waste Safety Target: Zero

Verification: This performance measure is defined as any release to the environment from the following activities: fuel facilities, nuclear material users, spent fuel storage and transportation, decommissioning, and low-level waste and high-level waste repository activities that exceed applicable regulations as defined in 10 CFR 20.2203(a)(3). A 30-day written report is required on such releases.

Should an event meeting this threshold occur, it would be reported to the NRC and/or Agreement States through a number of sources, but primarily through required licensee notifications. These events are summarized in event notifications and preliminary notifications, which are used to widely disseminate the information to internal and external stakeholders.

The fuel facilities, nuclear material users, spent fuel storage and transportation, decommissioning, and low-level waste, and high-level waste repository programs contain elements that verify the completeness and accuracy of licensee reports. The IMPEP also provides a mechanism to verify that Agreement States and NRC regions are consistently collecting and reporting such events, as received from the licensees, and entering them into NMED.

The NRC has taken a number of steps to improve the timeliness and completeness of materials event data. These steps include assessment of the NMED data during monthly staff reviews; emphasis and analysis during the IMPEP review; NMED training in HQ, the regions, and in Agreement States; and discussions at all Agreement State and CRCPD meetings.

Validation: The regulations in 10 CFR Part 20 provide standards for protection against radiation. There is a logical basis for tracking releases subject to the 30-day reporting requirement under 10 CFR 20.2203(a)(3)(ii) as a performance measure for ensuring the protection of the environment. The NRC's regulatory process, including licensing, inspection, guidance, regulations, and enforcement activities, is sufficient to ensure that releases of radioactive materials that exceed regulatory limits are infrequent.

In the unlikely event that a release to the environment exceeds regulatory limits, the NRC or Agreement State technical specialists or our consultants will confirm whether the criteria were met, with input provided by expert consultants, as necessary.

The NRC does not look at statistical sampling of data to determine results. Rather, all event data are reviewed to determine if the performance measure has been met. There are two important data limitations in determining this performance measure. These include delay time for receiving information and/or the failure of the NRC to become aware of an event that causes environmental impacts. The NRC regulations associated with event reporting include specific requirements for timely notifications; there is a lag time separating the occurrence of an event and the known consequences of an event.

The NRC believes the probability of not being aware of an event that causes a radio-logical release to the environment that exceeds applicable regulations is very small. Periodic licensee inspections and regulatory reporting requirements are sufficient to ensure that an event of this magnitude would become known.

If such an event occurred, it would result in a prompt and thorough investigation of the event, its consequences, its root causes, and the necessary actions by the licensee and the NRC to mitigate the situation and prevent recurrence. In addition to these immediate actions, the NRC holds periodic meetings, where staff and management validate the occurrence of these events.

Goal 2—Security: Ensure the secure use and management of radioactive materials.

Nuclear Reactor and Nuclear Materials and Waste Security

Strategic Outcome:

Prevent any instances where licensed radioactive materials are used domestically in a manner hostile to the security of the United States.

Performance Measures:

1 – Number of unrecovered losses or thefts of risk-significant radioactive sources.

Target: Zero

Verification: Under AO Criterion I.C.1, the agency counts any unrecovered lost, stolen, or abandoned sources that exceed the values listed in Appendix P, "Category 1 and 2 Radioactive Material," to 10 CFR Part 110, "Export and Import of Nuclear Equipment and Material." Excluded from reporting under this criterion are those events involving sources that are lost, stolen, or abandoned under certain conditions; specifically, (1) sources abandoned in accordance with the requirements of 10 CFR 39.77(c), (2) sealed sources contained in labeled, rugged source housings, (3) recovered sources with sufficient indication that doses in excess of the reporting thresholds specified in AO Criteria I.A.1 and I.A.2 did not occur during the time the source was missing, (4) unrecoverable sources lost under such conditions that doses in excess of the reporting thresholds specified in AO Criteria I.A.1 and I.A.2 were not known to have occurred, and (5) other sources that are lost or abandoned and declared unrecoverable, for which the agency has determined that the risk-significance of the source is low based on the location (e.g., water depth) or physical characteristics (e.g., half life, housing) of the source and its surroundings, where all reasonable efforts have been made to recover the source and where it has been determined that the source is not recoverable and would not be considered a realistic safety or security risk under this measure.

Verification: Losses or thefts of radioactive material greater than or equal to 1000 times the quantity specified in Appendix C, "Quantities of Licensed Material Requiring Labeling," to

10 CFR Part 20 must be reported (per 10 CFR 20.2201(a)) by telephone to the NRC HQ Operations Center or Agreement State immediately (interpreted as within 4 hours) if the licensee believes that an exposure could result to persons in unrestricted areas. If an event meeting the thresholds described above occurs, it would be reported through a number of sources but primarily through this required licensee notification. Events that are publicly available are then entered and tracked in NMED, which is an essential system used to collect and store information on such events. Separate methods are used to track events that are not publicly available. Additionally, licensees must meet the reporting and accounting requirements in 10 CFR Part 73, "Physical Protection of Plants and Materials," and 10 CFR Part 74.

The NRC's inspection programs are key elements in verifying the completeness and accuracy of licensee reports. The IMPEP also provides a mechanism to verify that Agreement States and the NRC regions are consistently collecting and reporting such events as received from the licensees and are entering these events in NMED. In some cases, upon receiving a report, the NRC or Agreement State initiates an independent investigation that verifies the reliability of the reported information. When performed, these investigations enable the NRC or Agreement State to verify the accuracy of the reported data.

The regulation in 10 CFR 20.2201(b) requires a 30-day written report for lost or stolen sources that are greater than or equal to 10 times the quantity specified in Appendix C to 10 CFR Part 20 if the source is still missing at that time. In addition, 10 CFR 20.2201(d) requires an additional written report within 30 days of a licensee learning any additional substantive information. The NRC interprets this requirement as including reporting recovery of sources.

The NRC issued guidance in the form of a regulatory information summary (RIS 2005-21) to clarify the current 10 CFR 20.2201(d) requirement for reporting recovery of a risk-significant source. The NRC asked the Agreement States to send copies of the RIS (or equivalent document) to their licensees. The NRC issued the NSTS final rule in November 2006. On January 31, 2009, NRC licensees and Agreement State licensees were required to begin reporting information on source transactions to the NSTS. Implementation of this system creates an inventory of risk-significant sources.

This rulemaking established reporting requirements for risk-significant sources (including reporting timeframes) by adding specific requirements to 10 CFR 20.2201, "Reports of Theft or Loss of Licensed Material," for risk-significant sources, including a requirement for licensees to report the recovery of a risk-significant source within 30 days of recovery.

Validation: Events collected under this performance measure are actual losses, thefts, or diversions of materials described above. Such events could compromise public health and safety, the environment, and the common defense and security. Events of this magnitude are expected to be rare. The information reported under 10 CFR Part 73 and 10 CFR Part 74 is required so that the NRC is aware of events that could endanger public health and safety or national security. Any failures at the level of the strategic plan would result in immediate investigation and followup.

If an event subject to the reporting requirements described above occurs, it would result in a prompt and thorough investigation of the event, its consequences, its root causes, and the necessary actions by the licensee, the NRC, and/or an Agreement State to mitigate the situation and prevent recurrence.

2-Number of substantiated cases of theft or diversion of licensed risk-significant radioactive sources or formula quantities of special nuclear material; or attacks that result in radiological sabotage.

Target: Zero

Verification: In AO Criterion I.C.2, "substantiated" means a situation that requires additional action by the agency or other proper authorities because of an indication of loss, theft, or unlawful diversion-such as an allegation of diversion, report of lost or stolen material, statistical processing difference, or other indication of loss of material control or accountability-that cannot be refuted following an investigation. A formula quantity of SNM is defined in 10 CFR 70.4. Radiological sabotage is defined in 10 CFR 73.2. Licensees subject to the requirements of 10 CFR Part 73 must call the NRC within 1 hour of an occurrence to report any breaches of security or other event that may potentially lead to theft or diversion of material or to sabotage at a nuclear facility. The NRC's safeguards requirements are described in 10 CFR 73.71, "Reporting of Safeguards Events"; Appendix G, "Reportable Safeguards Events," to 10 CFR Part 73; and 10 CFR 74.11, "Reports of Loss or Theft or Attempted Theft or Unauthorized Production of Special Nuclear Material." The information assessment team composed of NRC HQ and regional staff members would conduct an immediate assessment for any significant events to determine any further actions that are needed, including coordination with the intelligence community and law enforcement. In accordance with 10 CFR 73.71(d), the licensee must also file a written report within 60 days of the incident describing the event and the steps that the licensee took to protect the nuclear facility. This information will enable the NRC to adequately assess whether radiological sabotage has occurred.

Validation: Events subject to reporting requirements are those that endanger the public health and safety and the environment through deliberate acts of theft or diversion of material or through sabotage directed against the nuclear facilities that the agency licenses. Events of this type are extremely rare. If such an event occurs, it would result in a prompt and thorough investigation of the event, its consequences, its root causes, and the necessary actions by the licensee and/or the NRC to mitigate the situation and prevent recurrence. The investigation ensures the validity of the information and assesses the significance of the event.

3–Number of substantiated losses of formula quantities of special nuclear material or substantiated inventory discrepancies of a formula quantity of special nuclear material that are judged to be caused by theft, diversion, or by substantial breakdown of the accountability system.

Target: Zero

Verification: Licensees must record events associated with AO Criterion I.C.3 within 24 hours of the identified event in a safeguards log maintained by the licensee. The licensee must retain the log as a record for 3 years after the last entry is made or until termination of the license. The NRC relies on its safeguards inspection program to ensure the reliability of recorded data. The NRC makes a determination of whether a substantiated breakdown has resulted in a vulnerability to radiological sabotage, theft, diversion, or unauthorized enrichment of special nuclear material. When making substantiated breakdown determinations, the NRC evaluates the materials event data to ensure that licensees are reporting and collecting the proper event data.

Validation: "Substantiated" means a situation that requires additional action by the agency or other proper authorities because of an indication of loss, theft, or unlawful diversion-such as an allegation of diversion, report of lost or stolen material, statistical processing difference, other system breakdown closely related to the material control and accounting program (such as an item control system associated with the licensee's facility IT system), or other indication of loss of material control or accountability-that cannot be refuted following an investigation. A formula quantity of SNM is defined in 10 CFR 70.4. Events collected under this performance measure may indicate a vulnerability to radiological sabotage, theft, diversion, or loss of SNM. Such events could compromise public health and safety, the environment, and the common defense and security. The NRC relies on its safeguards inspection program to help validate the reliability of recorded data and determine whether a breakdown of a physical protection or material control and accounting system has actually resulted in vulnerability.

Target: Less than or equal to one

Verification: The AO Criterion I.C.4, a "substantial breakdown" is defined as a red finding in the security cornerstone of the ROP or significant performance problems and/or operational events resulting in a determination of overall unacceptable performance or in a shutdown condition (inimical to the effective functioning of the Nation's critical infrastructure). Radiological sabotage is defined in 10 CFR 73.2. Licensees are required to report to the NRC, immediately after the occurrence becomes known, any known breakdowns of physical security, based on the requirements in 10 CFR 73.71 and Appendix G to 10 CFR Part 73. If a licensee reports such an event, the HQ operations officer prepares an official record of the initial event report. The NRC begins responding to such an event immediately upon notification, with the activation of its information assessment team. A licensee must follow its initial telephone notification with a written report submitted to the NRC within 30 days.

The licensee records breakdowns of physical protection resulting in a vulnerability to radiological sabotage, theft, diversion, or loss of SNM or radioactive waste within 24 hours in a safeguards log maintained by the licensee. The licensee must retain the log as a record for 3 years after the last entry is made or until termination of the license. Licensees subject to

10 CFR Part 73 must also meet the reporting requirements detailed in 10 CFR 73.71. The NRC evaluates all of the reported events based on the criteria in 10 CFR 73.71 and Appendix G to 10 CFR Part 73. The NRC also maintains and relies on its safeguards inspection program to ensure the reliability of recorded and reported data.

Validation: Events assessed under this performance measure are those that threaten nuclear activities by deliberate acts, such as radiological sabotage, directed against facilities. If a licensee reports such an event, the information assessment team evaluates and validates the initial report and determines any further actions that may be necessary. Tracking breakdowns of physical security indicates whether the licensee is taking the necessary security precautions to protect the public, given the potential consequences of a nuclear accident attributable to sabotage or the inappropriate use of nuclear material either in this country or abroad.

Events collected under this performance measure may indicate a vulnerability to radiological sabotage, theft, diversion, or loss of SNM or radioactive waste. Such events could compromise public health and safety, the environment, and the common defense and security. The NRC relies on its safeguards inspection program to help validate the reliability of recorded data and determine whether a breakdown of a physical protection or material control and accounting system has actually resulted in a vulnerability.

5–Number of significant unauthorized disclosures of classified and/or safeguards information.

Target: Zero

Verification: With regard to AO Criterion I.C.5, any alleged or suspected violations by NRC licensees of the Atomic Energy Act, Espionage Act, or other Federal statutes related to classified or Safeguards Information must be reported to the NRC under the requirements of

10 CFR 95.57(a) (for classified information), 10 CFR Part 73 (for Safeguards Information), and NRC orders (for Safeguards Information subject to modified handling requirements). However, for performance reporting, the NRC would only count those disclosures or compromises that actually cause damage to national security or to public health and safety. Such events would be reported to the cognizant security agency (i.e., the security agency with jurisdiction) and the regional administrator of the appropriate NRC regional office, as listed in Appendix A, "U.S. Nuclear Regulatory Commission Offices and Classified Mailing Addresses," to 10 CFR Part 73. The regional administrator would then contact the Division of Security Operations at NRC HQ, which would assess the violation and notify other NRC offices and other government agencies, as appropriate. A determination would be made as to whether the compromise damaged national security or public health and safety. Any unauthorized disclosures or compromises of classified or Safeguards Information that damaged national security or public health and safety would result in immediate investigation and followup by the NRC. In addition, NRC inspections will verify that licensees' routine handling of classified and Safeguards Information (including Safeguards Information subject to modified handling requirements) conforms to established security information management requirements.

Any alleged or suspected violations of this performance measure by NRC employees, contractors, or other personnel would be reported in accordance with NRC procedures to the Director of Division of Facilities and Security at NRC HQ. The NRC maintains a strong system of controls over national security and Safeguards Information, including (1) annual required training for all employees, (2) safe and secure document storage, and (3) physical access control in the form of guards and badged access.

Validation: Events collected under this performance measure are unauthorized disclosures of classified or Safeguards Information that damage the national security or public health and safety. Events of this magnitude are not expected and would be rare. If such an event occurs, it would result in a prompt and thorough investigation, including consequences, root causes, and necessary actions by the licensees and the NRC to mitigate the consequences and prevent recurrence. NRC investigation teams also validate the materials event data to ensure that licensees are reporting and collecting the proper event data.

GOALS, PERFORMANCE MEASURE, AND PROGRAM CROSSWALK

The following table shows the relationship between the agency's goals, performance measures, and its seven program business lines. For example, the strategic outcome of "prevent the occurrence of any nuclear reactor accidents" relates to the New Reactors and Operating Reactors business lines. The strategic outcome of "prevent the occurrence of any inadvertent criticality events" relates to all of the agency's business lines. Each program evaluates event reports and other pertinent data to report the results for each strategic outcome, performance measure, and output measure. For each output measure, the specific product line involved is identified in the table.

Goals, Performance Measures, And Programs Crosswalk—Safety

Measures	NRC Business Lines						
	New Reactors	Operating Reactors	Fuel Facilities	Materials Users	HLW	Decomm & LLW	Spent Fuel
Strategic Outcomes							
Prevent the occurrence of any nuclear reactor accidents.	X	X	X				
Prevent the occurrence of any inadvertent criticality events.	X	X	X	X	X	X	X
Prevent the occurrence of any acute radiation exposures resulting in fatalities.	X	X	X	X	X	X	X
Prevent the occurrence of any releases of radioactive materials that result in significant radiation exposures.	X	X	X	X	X	X	X
Prevent the occurrence of any releases of radioactive materials that cause significant adverse environmental impacts.	X	X	X	X	X	X	X
Performance Measures							
Number of new conditions evaluated as red by the NRC's reactor oversight process.		X					
Number of significant ASPs of a nuclear reactor accident.		X					
Number of operating reactors whose integrated performance entered the Manual Chapter 0350 process, the multiple/ repetitive degraded or unacceptable cornerstone of the ROP Action Matrix with no performance exceeding AO Criteria.		X					
Number of significant adverse trends in industry safety performance.		X					

PERFORMANCE MEASUREMENT

Goals, Performance Measures, and Programs Crosswalk—Safety

Measures	New Reactors	Operating Reactors	Fuel Facilities	Materials Users	HLW	Decomm & LLW	Spent Fuel
			NRC Business Lines				
Number of events with radiation exposures to the public or occupational workers that exceed AO Criterion I.A.	x	x	x	x	x	x	x
Number of radiological releases to the environment that exceed applicable regulatory limits.	x	x	x	x	x	x	x
Output Measures							
Licensing actions completed per year.		Licensing					
Age of other licensing task Inventory.		Licensing					
Age of licensing action inventory		Licensing					
Other licensing tasks completed per year.		Licensing					
Number of operator licensing examinations administered.		Licensing					
Completion of license renewal application reviews.		Licensing					
Number of plants for which the baseline inspection program was completed during the most recently ended inspection cycle.		Oversight					
Timeliness of SDP evaluations.		Oversight					
Time to complete reviews of technical allegations.		Oversight					
Timeliness in completing enforcement actions.		Oversight					
Timeliness in completing investigations-Target 1.		Oversight					
Timeliness in completing investigations-Target 2		Oversight					
Timeliness in completing actions on critical research programs		Research					
Acceptable technical quality of agency research technical products.		Research					
Emergency Response Performance Index.		Event Response					
Efficiency measure: Transitioning from hard-copy distribution of outgoing licensee correspondence to electronic distribution		Licensing					
Efficiency measure: Revise inspection process		Oversight					

	NRC Business Lines						
Measures	New Reactors	Operating Reactors	Fuel Facilities	Materials Users	HLW	Decomm & LLW	Spent Fuel
Efficiency measure: Minimize necessary communication systems devices for senior manager use.		Oversight					
Review early site permit applications on the schedules negotiated with the applicants.	Licensing						
Review design certification applications on the schedules negotiated with the applicants.	Licensing						
Review combined license (COL) applications on the schedules negotiated with the applicants.	Licensing						
Prepare for the review of advanced reactor applications on schedules that support submittals of advanced reactor applications.	Licensing						
Review small modular reactor (SMR) design certification applications on the schedules negotiated with the applicants.	Licensing						
Identify and resolve policy and key technical issues facing the review small modular reactor (SMR) applications. Implement resolution through rule changes and/or guidance development.	Licensing						
Review SMR preapplication submittals on the schedules negotiated with the applicants.	Licensing						
Complete all vendor inspections as scheduled and resourced.	Oversight		Oversight				
Efficiency: Transition subsequent COL reviews from a 6-phase to a 4-phase approach.	Licensing						
Timeliness of completing "complex" fuel cycle licensing actions, from the date of acceptance, excluding request for additional information with an assumption of 30-day response to a request for additional information				Licensing			
Timeliness of completing "noncomplex" fuel cycle licensing actions (e.g., amendments and reviews) from the date of acceptance, including a 30-day response for a request for additional information				Licensing			

PERFORMANCE MEASUREMENT

Goals, Performance Measures, and Programs Crosswalk—Safety

Measures	NRC Business Lines						
	New Reactors	Operating Reactors	Fuel Facilities	Materials Users	HLW	Decomm & LLW	Spent Fuel
Safety and safeguards inspection modules. Complete all core and reactive inspect ion modules as scheduled in Fuel Cycle Master Inspection Plan				Oversight			
Timeliness of safety and safeguards inspection modules. Complete core inspection modules as scheduled in Fuel Cycle Master Inspection Plan				Oversight			
Timeliness in completing reviews for technical allegations.				Oversight			
Percentage of operating facilities for which the core inspection program was completed during the most recently ended inspection cycle.				Oversight			
Efficiency measure: New fuel facilities hearing support.				Licensing			
Timeliness of licensing actions- reviews of application for new materials licenses and license amendments.				Licensing			
Timeliness of licensing actions- reviews of application for materials license renewals and sealed source and device designs.				Licensing			
Timeliness of safety inspections of materials licensees				Oversight			
Timeliness in completing reviews for technical allegations				Oversight			
Timeliness in completing enforcement actions.				Oversight			
Timeliness in completing investigations - Target 1.				Oversight			
Timeliness in completing investigations-Target 2.				Oversight			
Percentage of materials and waste rulemakings completed on schedule.				Rule making			
Timeliness of completing actions on critical research programs.				Research			
Acceptable technical quality of agency research technical products.				Research			
Issuances of NRC import/export authorizations.				International Activities			

Goals, Performance Measures, and Programs Crosswalk—Safety

Measures	NRC Business Lines						
	New Reactors	Operating Reactors	Fuel Facilities	Materials Users	HLW	Decomm & LLW	Spent Fuel
Complete storage container and installation design reviews within timeliness goals.							Licensing
Complete transportation container design reviews within timeliness goals.							Licensing
Utilizing intra-agency contracting							Licensing
Number of spent fuel storage and transportation inspections completed							Oversight
Timeliness of completing actions on critical research programs.							Research
Acceptable technical quality of agency research technical products.							Research
Waste confidence and extended long-term storage activities-percent of planned products completed within a FY.							Research
Support program licensing activities by preparing and/or reviewing environmental reports and preparing environmental review documents.						Licensing	
Clean up complex materials, fuel cycle sites, and power reactors; complete uranium recovery licensing reviews.						Oversight	
Provide support to DOE for waste incidental to reprocessing (WIR) activities.						Oversight	
Timeliness of completing actions on critical research programs.						Research	
Acceptable technical quality of agency research technical products.						Research	
Provide support to IAEA Waste Safety Standards Committee reviews, consultancies/expert missions, Joint Convention, and Nuclear Energy Agency.						International Activities	
Eliminate the need for some site-specific EISs (i.e., by reducing resource needs) by developing a Generic Environmental Impact Statement (GEIS) for uranium recovery environmental reviews.						Licensing	

PERFORMANCE MEASUREMENT

Goals, Performance Measures, and Programs Crosswalk—Security							
Measures	**NRC Business Lines**						
	New Reactors	**Operating Reactors**	**Fuel Facilities**	**Materials Users**	**HLW**	**Decomm & LLW**	**Spent Fuel**
Strategic Outcome							
No instances where licensed radioactive materials are used domestically in a manner hostile to the security of the United States.	x	x	x	x	x	x	x
Performance Measures							
Unrecovered losses of risk-significant radioactive sources.	x	x	x	x	x	x	x
Number of substantiated cases of actual theft or diversion of licensed, risk-significant radioactive sources or formula quantities of SNM or attacks that result in radiological sabotage.	x	x	x	x	x	x	x
Number of substantiated losses of formula quantities of SNM or substantiated inventory discrepancies of formula quantities of SNM that are judged to be caused by theft or diversion or by substantial breakdown of the accountability system.	x	x	x	x	x	x	x
Number of substantial breakdowns of physical security or material control (i.e., access control, containment, or accountability systems) that significantly weakened the protection against theft, diversion, or sabotage.	x	x	x	x	x	x	x
Number of significant unauthorized disclosures of classified and/ or Safeguards Information.	x	x	x	x	x	x	x

OFFICE OF THE INSPECTOR GENERAL

OFFICE OF THE INSPECTOR GENERAL

NRC's OIG was established as a statutory entity on April 15, 1989, in accordance with the 1988 amendments to the Inspector General Act. The OIG mission is to (1) independently and objectively conduct and supervise audits and investigations relating to NRC programs and operations, (2) prevent and detect fraud, waste, and abuse, and (3) promote economy, efficiency, and effectiveness in NRC's programs and operations.

In addition, OIG reviews existing and proposed regulations, legislation, and directives and provides comments, as appropriate, and makes recommendations to the agency concerning their impact on the economy and efficiency of agency programs and operations. The Inspector General keeps the NRC Chairman and members of Congress informed about problems, recommends corrective actions, and monitors NRC's progress in implementing these actions.

Budget Overview Budget Authority by Program (Dollars In Millions)						
	FY 2012 Enacted		FY 2013 Request		Delta FY 2013–FY 2012	
Summary	$M	FTE	$M	FTE	$M	FTE
Program Support	1.276		1.392		0.116	
Program Salaries & Benefits	9.585	58.0	9.628	58.0	0.044	0.0
Total	$10.860	58.0	$11.020	58.0	$0.160	0.0

Numbers may not add due to rounding.

PROGRAM RESOURCE SUMMARY

The FY 2013 proposed budget request for the Office of the Inspector General is $11.020 million, which includes $9.628 million in salaries and benefits to support 58 FTE, and $1.392 million in contract support and travel. These resources will fund the activities for the Audits and Investigations Programs.

Budget Authority and Full-Time Equivalents by Program Budget Authority by Program (Dollars in Millions)						
	FY 2012 Enacted		FY 2013 Request		Delta FY 2013–FY 2012	
	$M	FTE	$M	FTE	$M	FTE
Summary						
Audits	7.171	37.0	7.308	37.0	0.137	0.0
Program Salaries and Benefits	3.689	21.0	3.712	21.0	0.023	0.0
Total	$10.860	58.0	$11.020	58.0	$0.160	0.0

Numbers may not add due to rounding.

In accordance with Office of Management and Budget (OMB) requirements, OIG is showing the full cost associated with its programs for the FY 2013 budget with the following caveat. As a result of an October 1989 memorandum of understanding between NRC's Chief Financial Officer and the Inspector General and a subsequent amendment in March 1991, OIG no longer requests that funding for some OIG management and support services be included in the OIG appropriation. It was agreed that funds for OIG infrastructure requirements and other agency support services would instead be included in NRC's main appropriation. For the most part, these costs are not readily severable. Thus, this funding continues to be included in NRC's main appropriation.

AUDITS PROGRAM

Audits Budget Authority by Program (Dollars in Millions)						
	FY 2012 Enacted		FY 2013 Request		Delta FY 2013–FY 2012	
	$M	FTE	$M	FTE	$M	FTE
Summary						
Program Support	7.121	37.0	7.308	37.0	0.137	0.0
Total	**$7.121**	37.0	**$7.308**	37.0	**$0.137**	0.0

Numbers may not add due to rounding.

Highlights

The OIG Audits Program focuses on the agency's management and financial operations; economy and efficiency with which an organization, program, or function is managed; and whether the programs achieve intended results. OIG auditors assess the degree to which an organization complies with laws, regulations, and internal policies in carrying out programs, and they test program effectiveness as well as the accuracy and reliability of financial statements. The overall objective of an audit is to identify ways to enhance agency operations and promote greater economy and efficiency.

For FY 2013, OIG requests $7.308 million and 37 FTE to carry out its Audits Program activities. With these resources, the Audits Program will conduct approximately 22 audits and evaluations. This will enable the OIG to provide coverage of NRC's Reactor Safety, Materials and Waste Safety, Security, and Corporate Support Programs. OIG's assessment of these mission-critical programs will support the agency in accomplishing its goals to ensure adequate protection of public health and safety and the environment, and in the secure use and management of radioactive materials.

Changes from FY 2012 Enacted

Resources increase in the Audits Program to fund the 0.5% provisional estimate for the January 2013 pay raise and acquire essential contract audit services.

FY 2012–FY 2013 Audits Program Performance Goals

> Safety Area: 85% of audit products/activities undertaken will identify critical risk areas or management challenges relating to the improvement of NRC's safety programs.

> Security Area: 90% of audit products/activities undertaken will identify critical risk areas or management challenges relating to the improvement of NRC's security programs.

> Corporate Management Area: 80% of audit products/activities undertaken will identify critical risk areas or management challenges relating to the improvement of NRC's corporate management programs.

> Eighty-five percent of completed audit products or activities will have a high impact on strengthening NRC's safety, security, and/or corporate management programs.

> Obtain agency agreement on at least 92% of OIG audit recommendations.

> Obtain final agency action on an aggregate of 70% of OIG audit recommendations within 2 years.

Selected FY 2011 Audits Program Accomplishments

In FY 2011, OIG issued 20 reports pertaining to NRC programs and operations. These reports either evaluate high-risk agency programs or comply with mandatory financial and computer security-related legislation.

Examples of Recently Completed Work are as Follows:

Audit of NRC's Implementation of 10 CFR Part 21, Reporting of Defects and Noncompliance:

The Energy Reorganization Act of 1974, as Amended, Section 206, Noncompliance, requires licensees that operate nuclear power plants to notify NRC of defects in basic components that could cause a substantial safety hazard. NRC uses Title 10, Code of Federal Regulations, *Part 21, Reporting of Defects and Noncompliance* (Part 21), to implement the provisions of Section 206. The audit objective was to determine if NRC's implementation of Federal regulations requiring reactor licensees to report defects contained in installed equipment is meeting the intent of the *Energy Reorganization Act of 1974, as Amended, Section 206, Noncompliance.*

Audit Results:

NRC staff has initiated action to better align NRC's defect reporting guidance with Section 206 of the Energy Reorganization Act. However, NRC will need to take further action so that NRC's implementation of Part 21 fully meets the intent of Section 206. Despite Section 206 requirements for licensees that operate nuclear power plants to notify NRC of defects in basic components that could cause a substantial safety hazard, NRC staff has noted Part 21 reporting issues, and OIG analysis of industry data indicates that there are apparent unreported Part 21 defects. Both NRC and OIG assessments identified events that had not been reported under Part

21, despite implications that such reporting may have been warranted. Unless NRC takes action to fully implement Section 206, staff and stakeholders may not be notified of component defects. Additionally, NRC inspectors face difficulties in enforcing defect reporting given the lack of clarity in Part 21 and related guidance.

Audit of NRC's Oversight of Master Materials Licensees:

NRC issues Master Materials Licenses (MMLs) to Federal agencies authorizing use of nuclear material at multiple sites that fall under the jurisdiction of the Federal agency. The MML allows the agency to conduct some activities as a regulator, such as issuing permits for sites that use materials (referred to as permittees), conducting inspections, and taking enforcement action. NRC provides oversight of MML licensees primarily through biennial reviews and of permittees through independent inspections. As of April 2011, NRC had issued MMLs to three Federal agencies: the Departments of the Air Force, Navy, and Veterans Affairs. The audit objective was to determine whether NRC's oversight of MML licensees adequately protects public health and safety and the environment.

Audit Results:

Over the past decade, NRC has made some improvements to its oversight of MML licensees; however, OIG identified three areas for NRC to further strengthen its oversight of this unique type of materials licensee. NRC management could strengthen MML licensee oversight by (1) improving the guidance for NRC staff providing technical assistance and training to MML licensees, (2) improving the guidance for the selection of MML permittees for NRC independent inspection, and (3) clarifying MML licensee regulatory oversight roles, responsibilities, and accountabilities.

Audit of NRC's Purchase Card Program:

The Governmentwide Purchase Card Program was established in the late 1980s as a way to streamline Federal acquisition processes by providing a low-cost, efficient vehicle for obtaining goods and services directly from vendors. Each Federal agency is required to develop and maintain written policies and procedures for the appropriate use of Government purchase cards. From December 1, 2008, through March 31, 2010, NRC had about 160 purchase cardholders who incurred transactions totaling approximately $8.3 million. The audit objective was to determine whether NRC has established and implemented an effective system of internal control over the use of Federal purchase cards.

Audit Results:

NRC employees are not consistently following agency Purchase Card Program guidance for closing purchase card accounts, tagging property bought with purchase cards, and requesting 30-day spending limit increases. Furthermore, employees appear to be making split transactions to circumvent cardholder single transaction limits and using convenience checks improperly, which results in unnecessary cost to the Government. In addition, NRC does not maintain complete records of NRC purchase cardholders, which may result in agency staff not having the proper authority to use purchase cards and write convenience checks. Addressing these concerns will strengthen NRC's internal control over Federal purchase cards.

Two Audits of NRC's Oversight of Independent Spent Fuel Storage Installations (ISFSIs): Safety and Security:

With the anticipated growth of nuclear power in the United States and the uncertainty over the permanent storage of spent fuel at Yucca Mountain, nuclear power plants have a growing need for additional spent fuel storage capacity to support continued operation. ISFSIs are NRC-licensed facilities that store dry casks containing used nuclear reactor fuel, otherwise known as spent fuel. Most ISFSIs are located at operating reactor sites. An ISFSI typically consists of a concrete storage pad, storage containers (casks), and any support facilities. OIG conducted two audits related to ISFSI safety and security. The ISFSI safety audit objective was to determine if NRC has the requisite processes in place for reviewing ISFSI safety. The ISFSI security audit objective was to determine the adequacy of NRC's oversight of ISFSI security.

Audit Results:

OIG identified opportunities for improvement in ISFSI safety and security. Auditors found that there is no formalized agencywide training program for ISFSI safety inspectors, who lack a consistent understanding of inspection requirements. Auditors also identified a variance of 1 to almost 6 years between routine ISFSI inspections because routine inspection frequency has not been clearly defined in inspection guidance. With regard to security, although three NRC offices play key ISFSI security roles, there is no overarching process document describing these roles and responsibilities, which allows for lapses involving shared responsibilities. NRC does not have a comprehensive ISFSI security inspection procedure that includes a defined frequency for the inspections or a formal ISFSI security inspector qualification program to ensure that inspectors are trained in both security and ISFSI systems and equipment. NRC also lacks a centralized repository of relevant ISFSI security information. Instead, the agency maintains such information in multiple database systems in a manner that does not facilitate easy retrieval.

Examples of Ongoing Audit Work are as Follows:

Audit of NRC's Process for Evaluating the Relevance of Inspections, Tests, Analyses, and Acceptance Criteria (ITAAC):

When licensing a plant under Title 10, Code of Federal Regulations (10 CFR), Part 52, NRC is required to verify, within the combined license application, the ITAAC that, if met, are sufficient to provide reasonable assurance that the facility has been constructed and will be operated in conformity with the license, the provisions of the Atomic Energy Act, and the Commission's rules and regulations. Prior to the implementation of 10 CFR Part 52, the agency identified the ITAAC needed to issue a combined license for a new nuclear power facility. However, given the changes to the nuclear industry since the inception of 10 CFR Part 52, there are concerns that ITAAC may not provide NRC with all of the necessary information needed to make its licensing decisions. The audit objective is to assess NRC's regulatory approach, through the ITAAC review process, to ensure that new nuclear power plants have been constructed and will be operated in conformity with the license, the provisions of the Atomic Energy Act, and Commission's rules and regulations.

Audit of Agency Use of Confirmatory Action Letters:

While auditing NRC's management of licensee commitments, OIG reviewed the implementation of several types of commitments, including those in Confirmatory Action Letters (CALs). A CAL is a letter issued to a licensee or vendor to emphasize and confirm the licensee's or vendor's agreement to take certain actions in response to specific issues. NRC's Enforcement Manual specifies that the level of significance of the issues addressed in a CAL should be such that if a licensee did not agree to meet the commitments in the nonlegally binding CAL, then the staff would likely proceed to issue an order, which is legally binding. Given the possible wide range of purposes to issue a CAL and the number of offices potentially involved in issuing a CAL, it is important the NRC implements this regulatory tool consistently. The audit objective is to determine the effectiveness of NRC's utilization of CALs as an extra-regulatory tool.

Audit of NRC's Oversight of Radiography Sources:

Radiography uses radiation to produce images of a subject, especially the internal features of a subject. For example, industrial radiography enables detection of internal physical imperfections such as voids, cracks, and flaws in welds, piping, and other components and structures. It is routinely used for examination of oil and gas pipelines, boilers, and pressure vessels. Radiography devices are often portable and subject to theft, loss, and damage. Each year, radiography devices, including their sources, are lost, stolen, or abandoned. The sources in these devices are of great concern because they are made from Cobalt-60, Iridium-192, or other highly radioactive material that can be lethal even in small amounts. For example, one gram of Cobalt-60 will cause a lethal exposure to anyone exposed for 1 hour or more at 1 meter or closer. The audit objective is to determine the adequacy of NRC's processes for overseeing license activities addressing the safety and control of radiography sources.

	Investigations Budget Authority by Program (Dollars in Millions)					
	FY 2012 Enacted		FY 2013 Request		Delta FY 2013–FY 2012	
	$M	FTE	$M	FTE	$M	FTE
Summary						
Program Support	3.689	21.0	3.712	21.0	0.023	0.0
Total	$3.689	21.0	$3.712	21.0	$0.023	0.0

Numbers may not add due to rounding.

Highlights

OIG's responsibility for detecting and preventing fraud, waste, and abuse within NRC includes investigating possible violations of criminal statutes relating to NRC programs and activities, investigating misconduct by NRC employees, interfacing with the Department of Justice on OIG-related criminal matters, and coordinating investigations and other OIG initiatives with Federal, State, and local investigative agencies and other OIGs. Investigations may be initiated as a result of allegations or referrals from private citizens; licensee employees; NRC employees; Congress; other Federal, State, and local law enforcement agencies; OIG audits; the OIG hotline; and Inspector General initiatives directed at bearing a high potential for fraud, waste, and abuse.

For FY 2013, OIG requests $3.712 million and 21 FTE to carry out its Investigations Program activities. Reactive investigations into allegations of criminal and other wrongdoing will continue to claim priority on OIG's use of available resources. Because NRC's mission is to protect the health and safety of the public, the Investigations Program's main concentration of effort and resources will involve investigations of alleged NRC staff misconduct that could adversely impact matters related to health and safety. OIG has also implemented a series of proactive initiatives designed to identify specific high-risk areas that are most vulnerable to fraud, waste, and abuse. With these resources, OIG will conduct approximately 60 investigations and Event Inquiries covering a broad range of allegations concerning misconduct and mismanagement affecting various NRC programs.

Changes from FY 2012 Enacted

Resources increase in the Investigations Program to fund the 0.5% provisional estimate for the January 2013 pay raise.

FY 2012–FY 2013 Investigations Program Performance Goals

> Safety Area: 85% of investigation products/activities undertaken will identify critical risk areas or management challenges relating to the improvement of NRC's safety programs.

> Security Area: 90% of investigation products/activities undertaken will identify critical risk areas or management challenges relating to the improvement of NRC's security programs.

> Corporate Management Area: 80% of investigation products/activities undertaken will identify critical risk areas or management challenges relating to the improvement of NRC's corporate management programs.

> Eighty-five percent of investigations or activities completed will have a high impact on strengthening NRC's safety, security, and/or corporate management programs.

> Obtain 90% agency action in response to OIG investigative reports.

> Complete 90% of active cases in less than 18 months on average.

Selected FY 2011 Investigations Program Accomplishments

In FY 2011, OIG completed 45 investigations and Event Inquiries. These investigative efforts are focused on violations of law or misconduct by NRC employees and contractors and allegations of irregularities or inadequacies in NRC programs and operations.

Examples of Recently Completed Work are as Follows:

Potential Conflict of Interest between the NRC and Contractors/Subcontractors Utilized by the Information Systems Laboratories, Inc.:

OIG conducted an investigation into an allegation concerning the legality of an NRC contract with Information Systems Laboratories, Inc. (ISL), a company that was contracted to review license applications submitted to NRC by utility companies requesting to build new nuclear power plants. This investigation addressed (1) whether NRC's contract with ISL involves activities that are inherently governmental and therefore should be performed by NRC employees, and (2) whether ISL was free of organizational conflicts of interest as it conducts reviews of highly technical issues that license applicants have also contracted out to evaluate as part of their applications to the NRC.

The Federal Acquisitions Regulations Subpart 7.5 prescribes policies and procedures to ensure that inherently governmental functions are not performed by contractors. "Inherently governmental function" means, as a matter of policy, a function that is so intimately related to the public interest as to mandate performance by Government employees. The Standards for Evaluation of Potential Conflict of Interest are prescribed in 48 CFR 2009.570-3(b)(1) and are used to determine whether there are conflicting roles that might bias an offeror's or contractor's judgment in relation to their work with the Government and ensure that the offeror or contractor is not given an unfair competitive advantage based on the performance of the contract.

In 2007, NRC entered into a 5-year, $33,852,575 contract with ISL to provide technical expertise and assistance in support of design certification, early site permit, combined license, environmental, and preapplication activities related to new reactor license applications for the Westinghouse AP1000 design. According to the NRC statement of work, the agency did not have the ability to complete the technical reviews of all the license applications in a productive and efficient manner. Thus, ISL would be required to support all the technical facets of new reactor licensing reviews.

Investigative Results:

This investigation determined that the contract work NRC requested from ISL was not an inherently governmental function because (1) ISL contractors and subcontractors serve as technical assistants, (2) NRC staff reviews all tasks completed by the contractor employees, and (3) NRC staff makes the decisions relative to the license applications.

The investigation also determined that there was no conflict of interest posed by NRC utilizing ISL contractor and subcontractor employees as subject matter experts who had also previously assisted licensees with their new reactor applications. OIG compared the names and employment dates of four new reactor license applicants who had submitted applications to NRC as of April 17, 2009, with the names of all ISL contractor and subcontractor employees involved in the review of the new reactor license applications on behalf of NRC. OIG found that, although contractor and subcontractor employees were working for ISL to review new reactor applications on behalf of the NRC, they were not reviewing the same applications that they helped to prepare.

NRC Actions Concerning Licensee Statements Regarding Adequacy of Decommissioning Trust Fund Balances:

OIG conducted an investigation into an allegation submitted by a private citizen to NRC under Title 10 Code of Federal Regulations (CFR) Section 2.206, which permits any person to file a petition requesting that the NRC take enforcement-related action (i.e., to modify, suspend, or revoke a license or to take other appropriate action). The 2.206 petition must be in writing and provide the grounds for taking the proposed action.

According to the petition filed by the private citizen, NRC knowingly allowed Entergy to lie about the amount of money in its decommissioning trust fund for three of its utilities: Vermont Yankee, River Bend, and Indian Point nuclear power plants. The citizen also alleged that he was personally lied to by NRC staff in a letter dated December 17, 2009, which stated, "only the decommissioning trust funds for Entergy's Vermont Yankee and River Bend nuclear power plants do not currently meet the funding levels of 10 CFR 50.75." The person alleged that Indian Point Unit 2 also had a funding shortfall; thus, the letter he received was inaccurate.

Title 10 CFR 50.75 requires a licensee to provide every 2 years a report on the state of its decommissioning trust fund. The purpose of the fund is to provide reasonable assurance that a licensee has sufficient funds to pay for the cleanup and removal of all nuclear and radiological material from the site. Regardless of the amount of money in the fund, a licensee is considered compliant as long as the report is filed.

Investigative Results:

OIG found no evidence to substantiate the claim that Entergy lied about the state of its decommissioning trust fund and no evidence that NRC staff knowingly allowed the company to lie. OIG also found that NRC's letter, dated December 17, 2009, accurately reflected the state of Entergy's decommissioning trust fund.

Conflicting Statements on NRC Policy Regarding Release of Cancer Treatment Patients to Hotels:

OIG conducted an investigation into an allegation that the NRC Office of the General Counsel (OGC) issued conflicting statements addressing the recovery of cancer treatment patients in hotels. In April 2008, OGC concurred with an Office of Federal and State Materials and Environmental Management Programs (FSME) Technical Assistance Request (TAR) response sent to Region I that stated the release of cancer treatment patients "to a hotel was not prohibited by [NRC] regulations." However, in November 2008, OGC filed a legal brief with the U.S. Court of Appeals for the Ninth Circuit (Ninth Circuit Court of Appeals) that stated, "NRC's rule [10 CFR Part 35.75] does not permit or encourage doctors to send treated patients to hotels." The NRC legal brief had been filed in response to a petitioner's challenge of NRC's denial of his request for rulemaking concerning the standards for release of patients treated with unsealed byproduct material. OIG also investigated whether NRC's legal brief to the Ninth Circuit Court of Appeals mischaracterized comments the petitioner submitted to NRC during the 10 CFR 35.75 rulemaking petition process.

Investigative Results:

OIG found that the FSME and OGC statements describing NRC's 10 CFR Part 35.75 patient release criteria give contradictory impressions. On face value, neither statement accurately reflects the actual language in the rule, which makes no mention of release destination. However, the TAR response contained background and explanatory information to connect the statement with the language. In contrast, the subheading used in OGC's legal brief contained no explanatory material and could be misunderstood as suggesting that the rule prohibits release to a hotel when this is not so.

OIG found that NRC's written legal brief to the Ninth Circuit Court of Appeals accurately characterized the petitioner's 10 CFR Part 35.75 petition for rulemaking comments with regard to his correction to the record. During an OGC attorney's oral argument on the same matter before the court, the attorney referred twice to the petitioner's having recanted information in his petition for rulemaking comments. In the first exchange, the attorney correctly described that the petitioner had recanted the source of his information that cancer treatment patients were going to hotels. In the second exchange, which occurred soon after the first, the attorney was interrupted by a judge before finishing his sentence; therefore, his characterization of the petitioner's comments was incomplete.

Alleged Flawed License Renewal Process by NRC Division of License Renewal:

OIG conducted an investigation into an allegation by a former NRC employee who questioned NRC's Division of License Renewal (DLR) process for issuing a Supplemental Environmental Impact Statement (SEIS) for both the Hope Creek and Salem Units 1 and 2 nuclear power plants. Since the nuclear power plants reside adjacent to each other, NRC management decided that only one SEIS would be produced. The license renewal process is generally a 30-month process from the time the licensee's renewal application is received until a decision is made on the renewal. One aspect of the license renewal is the development of the draft SEIS, which is required under the National Environmental Policy Act of 1969. The former employee alleged that the DLR project schedule for the SEIS is not ideal for this type of lengthy review process. The alleger also maintained that DLR management is pushing staff to complete these reviews, and the process yields inaccuracies. Further, there were concerns with the overall accuracy of the Salem/Hope Creek SEIS findings.

Investigative Results:

OIG found that the project schedule and review process for the SEIS projects are not unreasonable and are typically scheduled for completion in 18 to 22 months. OIG's review of the NRC internal Web site for reactor license renewal applications indicated that between January 2003 and the present, the average time to complete an SEIS was 18 months, but that there have been instances where final SEISs have been issued up to 32 months after receipt of the licensee's license renewal application. OIG found that the Environmental Protection Agency reviewed the draft SEIS for Salem/Hope Creek and determined it to be an excellent report.

Alleged Contract Fraud by Pacific Northwest National Laboratory:

OIG conducted an investigation involving alleged fraud in connection with work performed for NRC under DOE laboratory agreements with Pacific Northwest National Laboratory (PNNL). According to the allegation, two of the tasks being performed by PNNL listed the same deliverable, there were errors in the vouchers and missing vouchers for one task, and there were numerous problems with deliverables and deliverable dates.

Investigative Results:

OIG did not identify any instances of fraud in connection with PNNL's performance of the tasks. Although progress on the tasks fell behind schedule, NRC project managers for the tasks were informed about progress on the tasks, aware of the delays, and satisfied with the quality of the work performed and deliverables. Furthermore, the current NRC project manager and NRC technical advisor for the tasks were satisfied with PNNL's performance of the work. OIG also found that NRC requests for additional PNNL work during this time period contributed to some delays in completion of the work.

Examples of Ongoing Investigative Work are as Follows:

NRC Network Intrusion, Computer Misuse, and Computer Forensic Support:

The OIG Cyber Crime Unit conducts investigations into internal and external cyber breaches to the NRC's IT infrastructure, conducts cyber investigations involving the NRC and its employees, and works jointly with NRC staff to identify unauthorized or unknown activity on the NRC network. Investigations include computer misuse by NRC employees, targeted spear phishing attacks against NRC employees, attempted network intrusions, unauthorized release of electronic sensitive information, and forensic assistance to the NRC regarding alleged licensees' violations of regulatory requirements.

Review of NRC Grants To Identify Potential Grant Fraud:

OIG has an ongoing proactive initiative to review NRC grants awarded to various universities through the NRC Grants Program to develop programs in support of nuclear education or awards of scholarships to students to pursue either higher education or employment within the nuclear industry. OIG also has several current investigations involving alleged fraud pertaining to universities that receive NRC grants.

Review of NRC Licensee Supply Chain Vulnerabilities:

OIG has a proactive initiative to identify counterfeit, fraudulent, and suspect items (CSFI) that are either wittingly or unwittingly provided to nuclear utility companies within the nuclear acquisition supply chain. This investigative initiative is being coordinated with the Office of the National Counterintelligence Executive, and is aimed at identifying CSFI that enter into the nuclear supply chain when acquired by NRC licensee prime and subprime vendors.

OIG'S STRATEGIC GOALS, STRATEGIES, AND ACTIONS

OIG carries out its mission through its Audits and Investigations Programs. The FY 2008–2013 NRC-OIG Strategic Plan features three goals and guides the activities of these programs. The plan identifies the major challenges and risk areas facing the NRC and generally aligns with the agency's mission. It also includes a number of supporting strategies and actions that describe OIG's planned accomplishments over the strategic planning period. OIG's strategic plan can be found in its entirety at the following address: http://www.nrc.gov/insp-gen/plandocs/strategic-plan.pdf.

Through annual planning activities, audit and investigative resources focus on assessing NRC's safety, security, and corporate management programs involving the major challenges and risk areas facing the NRC in the given budget year. The work performed by OIG auditors and investigators is mutually supportive and complementary in pursuit of these objectives. Below are OIG's strategic goals and strategies covering this budget cycle.

OIG Strategic Goals

❯ Strategy 1-1: Identify risk areas associated with NRC's Reactor Oversight Process and make recommendations, as warranted, for addressing them.

❯ Strategy 1-2: Identify risk areas associated with NRC efforts to (1) prepare for and manage the review of applications for new power reactors, and (2) oversee construction of new power reactors to verify that they are built in conformance with approved designs and in compliance with approved construction standards and make recommendations, as warranted, for addressing them.

❯ Strategy 1-3: Identify risk areas facing the materials programs and make recommendations, as warranted, for addressing them.

❯ Strategy 1-4: Identify risk areas associated with low-level waste and the prospective licensing of the high-level waste repository and make recommendations, as warranted, for addressing them.

NRC continues to face a number of challenges in ensuring the public is protected from improper use of nuclear materials and technology. NRC, in concert with other agencies, must maintain a comprehensive assessment of threats and effectively integrate security considerations into its regulatory process. NRC must also ensure that security is adequately incorporated into the design and construction of new facilities. Below are OIG's strategies to support the NRC in facing these and other security-related challenges.

❯ Strategy 2-1: Identify risk areas involved in effectively securing both operating and proposed nuclear power plants, nuclear fuel cycle facilities, and nuclear materials and make recommendations, as warranted, for addressing them.

❯ Strategy 2-2: Identify risks associated with Emergency Preparedness and make recommendations, as warranted, for addressing them.

❯ Strategy 2-3: Identify challenges involved in responding to incidents and make recommendations, as warranted, for addressing them.

❯ Strategy 2-4: Identify evolving threats to NRC security and make recommendations, as warranted, for addressing them.

❯ Strategy 2-5: Identify risks associated with nonproliferation of nuclear material and nuclear technology and make recommendations, as warranted, for addressing them.

Strategic Goal 3: Increase the economy, efficiency, and effectiveness with which NRC manages and exercises stewardship over its resources.

NRC faces significant challenges to efficiently, effectively, and economically manage its resources. Although a number of organizational changes have been implemented in recent years, more changes will occur over the strategic timeframe. The agency will need to continue balancing workloads and priorities to support new reactor licensing efforts. This will create tremendous pressure on all program management areas, including human resources management, information technology, and financial management. Below is OIG's strategy to support the agency in mitigating these challenges .

> Strategy 3-1: Identify areas of corporate management risk within NRC and make recommendations, as warranted, for addressing them.

OIG Strategic Goal 1: Strengthen NRC's Efforts to Protect Public Health and Safety and the Environment

	2008	2009	2010	2011	2012	2013
Measure 1. Percentage of OIG products/activities[1] undertaken to identify risk areas or management challenges[2] relating to the improvement of NRC's safety programs.						
Target	80%	80%	85%	85%	85%	85%
Actual	100%	100%	100%	100%	TBD	TBD
Measure 2. Percentage of OIG products/activities that have a high impact[3] on improving NRC's safety program.						
Target	70%	70%	85%	85%	85%	85%
Actual	100%	89%	100%	90.9%	TBD	TBD
Measure 3. Number of audit recommendations agreed to by agency.						
Target	90%	90%	92%	92%	92%	92%
Actual	93%	60%[4]	60%[5]	80%[6]	TBD	TBD
Measure 4. Final agency action within 1 year of audit recommendations.						
Target	50%	50%	70%[7]	70%	70%	70%
Actual	63%	67%	80%	80%	TBD	TBD
Measure 5. Agency action in response to investigative reports.						
Target	90%	90%	90%	95%	95%	95%
Actual	100%	100%	100%	100%	TBD	TBD
Measure 6. Complete active cases in less than 18 months on average.						
Target					90%[8]	90%
Actual						TBD

1 The OIG products are issued as OIG reports. For the Audits Program, these are audit reports and evaluations. For the Investigations Program, these are investigations, Event Inquiries, and special inquiries. Activities are the OIG hotline or proactive investigative reports.

2 Congress left the determination and threshold of what constitutes a most serious challenge to the discretion of the Inspectors General. As a result, OIG applied the following definition: Serious management challenges are mission-critical areas or programs that have a potential for a perennial weakness or vulnerability that, without substantial management attention, would seriously impact agency operations or strategic goals.

3 High impact is the effect of an issued report or activity undertaken that results in: (a) confirming risk areas or management challenges that caused the agency to take corrective action, (b) real dollar savings or reduced regulatory burden, (c) identifying significant wrongdoing by individuals that results in criminal or administrative action, (d) clearing an individual wrongly accused, or (e) identifying regulatory actions or oversight that may have contributed to the occurrence of a specific event or incident or resulted in a potential adverse impact on public health or safety.

4 The agency required more than 90 days to review 5 of 6 recommendations on the Agreement State Program audit before resolution. Three of the 5 recommendations were agreed to within 98 days.

5 The agency required more than 90 days to review 4 recommendations on the Quality Assurance Planning for New Reactors audit prior to resolution. Subsequently, all 4 recommendations have been closed or resolved.

6 The agency required more than 90 days to review 3 of 5 recommendations on the Audit of NRC's Implementation of 10 CFR Part 21 on Reporting of Defects and Noncompliance. Subsequently, all 5 recommendations have been resolved.

7 The measure changed from final agency action within 1 year on audit recommendations to 2 years on audit recommendations starting in FY 2010.

8 Starting in FY 2012, OIG will measure the percentage of active cases completed in less than 18 months on average.

OFFICE OF THE INSPECTOR GENERAL

OIG Strategic Goal 2: Enhance NRC's Efforts to Increase Security in Response to an Evolving Threat Environment

	2008	2009	2010	2011	2012	2013
Measure 1. Percentage of OIG products/activities undertaken to identify critical risk areas or management challenges relating to the improvement of NRC's security programs.						
Target	85%	85%	90%	90%	90%	90%
Actual	100%	100%	100%	100%	TBD	TBD
Measure 2. Percentage of OIG products/activities that have a high impact on improving NRC's security program.						
Target	70%	70%	75%	75%	75%	75%
Actual	100%	100%	100%	100%	TBD	TBD
Measure 3. Number of audit recommendations agreed to by agency.						
Target	90%	90%	92%	92%	92%	92%
Actual	100%	82%[9]	96.6%	96.6%	TBD	TBD
Measure 4. Final agency action within 1 year of audit recommendations.						
Target	65%	65%	65%	70%[10]	70%	70%
Actual	70%	40%[11]	80%	80%	TBD	TBD
Measure 5. Agency action in response to investigative reports.						
Target	90%	90%	90%	90%	90%	90%
Actual	100%	100%	100%	100%	TBD	TBD
Measure 6. Complete active cases in less than 18 months on average.						
Target					90%[12]	90%
Actual					TBD	TBD

9 The agency took more than 90 days to review 2 recommendations on the National Source Tracking System audit. The agency agreed to both recommendations within 97 days.

10 The measure changed from final agency action within 1 year on audit recommendations to 2 years on audit recommendations starting in FY 2010.

11 The agency is taking more than 1 year to complete final action on recommendations related to information security. The agency agreed with all recommendations and action has been taken to correct identified deficiencies.

12 Starting in FY 2012, OIG will measure the percentage of active cases completed in less than 18 months on average.

OIG Strategic Goal 3: Improve the Economy, Efficiency, and Effectiveness with Which NRC Manages and Exercises Stewardship over its Resources

	2008	2009	2010	2011	2012	2013
Measure 1. Percentage of OIG products/activities undertaken to identify critical risk areas or management challenges relating to the improvement of NRC's resources stewardship.						
Target	65%	65%	80%	80%	80%	80%
Actual	100%	100%	100%	100%	TBD	TBD
Measure 2. Percentage of OIG products/activities that have a high impact on improving NRC's resources stewardship.						
Target	70%	70%	85%	85%	85%	85%
Actual	100%	92%	69.6%[13]	69.6%[14]	TBD	TBD
Measure 3. Number of audit recommendations agreed to by the agency.						
Target	90%	90%	90%	92%	92%	92%
Actual	100%	96%	100%	100%	TBD	TBD
Measure 4. Final agency action within 1 year of audit recommendations.						
Target	65%	65%	70%[15]	70%	70%	70%
Actual	53%[16]	54%[17]	92.9%	92.9%	TBD	TBD
Measure 5. Agency action in response to investigative reports.						
Target	90%	90%	90%	90%	90%	90%
Actual	100%	100%	100%	100%	TBD	TBD
Measure 6. Acceptance by NRC's Office of the General Counsel of OIG-referred Program Fraud and Civil Remedies Act cases.						
Target	70%	70%[18]				
Actual	No referrals	No referrals				
Measure 7. Complete active cases in less than 18 months on average.						
Target					90%[19]	90%
Actual					TBD	TBD

13 For FY 2010, a more rigorous standard was applied for the impact of investigations in the corporate management arena.

14 For FY 2011, a more rigorous standard was applied for the impact of investigations in the corporate management arena.

15 The measure changed from final agency action within 1 year on audit recommendations to 2 years on audit recommendations starting in FY 2010.

16 The majority of these audit recommendations pertain to the Technical Training Center audit recommendations audit that took longer for the agency to implement.

17 The agency is taking more than 1 year to complete final action on 12 of 17 Training and Development audit recommendations. The agency agreed with all recommendations and final action has been completed on all 17 recommendations.

18 The Performance measure was determined to be ineffective since another NRC program office was primarily responsible for ensuring completion of action with minimal activity from year to year and the measure will be removed starting in FY 2010.

19 Starting in FY 2012, OIG will measure the percentage of active cases completed in less than 18 months on average.

Verification and Validation of Measured Values and Performance

OIG uses an automated management information system to capture program performance data for the Audits and Investigations Programs. The integrity of the system was thoroughly tested and validated before implementation. Reports generated by the system provide both detailed information and summary data. Beginning with FY 2006, statistics for the Audits and Investigations Programs were fully integrated into the new system and used to compile OIG statistical performance data. All system data are deemed reliable.

Program Evaluations (Peer Reviews)

Independent quality assurance reviews undertaken in FY 2010 and FY 2011 determined that audits were conducted in conformance with the Government Accountability Office's Government Auditing Standards. An independent audit peer review performed in FY 2009 found that the Audits Program's system of quality control provided reasonable assurance that audits were conducted in accordance with applicable professional standards.

In addition, an independent investigative peer review was conducted in FY 2010 of the OIG Investigations Program. The program was found to be in compliance with the Council of Inspectors General on Integrity and Efficiency and Department of Justice investigative standards.

INSPECTOR GENERAL REFORM ACT CERTIFICATION FOR FY 2013

In accordance with the Inspector General Reform Act (Public Law 110-409), NRC OIG budget request that was submitted to the NRC Chairman for FY 2013 was for $11.020 million and 58 FTE and was subsequently approved. The Inspector General certifies that NRC's OIG training request of $120,000 satisfies the training requirements for the Inspector General's office. In addition, sufficient funds are available in the FY 2013 budget request to include the necessary funding resources to support the Council of Inspectors General on Integrity and Efficiency.

The following table depicts the relationship of the Inspector General program and associated resource requirements to OIG strategic goals.

FY 2013 Office of the Inspector General Budget Resources Linked to Strategic Goals			
	OIG Strategic Goals		
Program Links to Strategic Goals	Strengthen NRC's Public Health & Safety Efforts	Enhance NRC's Security Efforts	Increase NRC's Resource Stewardship Efforts
FY 2013 Programs ($11,020,000; 58 FTE)			
Audits ($7,308,000; 37 FTE)	$3,106,000 18.5 FTE	$1,237,000 6.5 FTE	$2,965,000 12.0 FTE
Investigations ($3,712,000; 21 FTE)	$1,445,000 8.0 FTE	$618,000 3.5 FTE	$1,649,000 9.5 FTE

Numbers may not add due to rounding.

MANAGEMENT AND OPERATIONAL SUPPORT

OIG's Management and Operational Support staff consists of senior managers, the general counsel, and an administrative support staff. OIG's senior managers will provide the continued vision, strategic direction, and guidance regarding the conduct and supervision of audits and investigations. Senior management will also ensure accountability regarding OIG's established goals and strategies and achievement of intended results.

In furtherance of OIG's mission to promote economy and efficiency, and to prevent fraud, waste, and abuse in agency programs and operations, OIG's general counsel, in coordination with cognizant OIG staff, will conduct analyses of existing and proposed legislation, regulations, directives, and policy issues. These objective analyses will result in timely written commentaries to the agency that prospectively identify and prevent potential problems.

The administrative support staff will assist OIG programs by providing independent personnel services; information technology and information management support; financial management, policy, and strategic planning support; training coordination; and the publication of OIG's Semiannual Report to Congress in accordance with the requirements of the Inspector General Act.

To carry out the functions of this program in FY 2013, OIG estimates that its costs will be $1,399,000, which includes salaries and benefits for 8 FTE. The tables below provide a breakdown of the FY 2013 budget estimates for Management and Operational Support by program and a cost comparison by function

.

OFFICE OF THE INSPECTOR GENERAL

Allocation Of Support Costs To OIG Programs

Management and Operational Support Allocation by Program ($K)	FY 2013 FTE	FY 2013 Salaries and Benefits	FY 2013 Contract and Support
Audits	5	830	45
Investigations	3	498	26
Total	8	$1,328	$71

Numbers may not add due to rounding.

Comparative Costs Of Management And Operational Support

Summary	FY 2011 Enacted	FY 2013 Request[20]
Budget Authority by Function ($K)		
Salaries and Benefits	1322	1328
Contract Support and Travel	68	71
Total Budget Authority	$1,390	$1,399
FTE	8	8

Numbers may not add due to rounding.

20 The OIG Management and Operational Support staff consists of senior managers, a general counsel, and administrative support personnel. To carry out the function of this program for FY 2013, OIG estimates its costs to be $1.399 million, which includes salaries and benefits for 8 FTE. The associated FTE and salaries and benefits estimate and contract support and travel estimates were allocated in proportion to each program's FTE percentage.

APPENDIX I
BUDGET AUTHORITY
BY FUNCTION

APPENDIX I:

The U.S. Nuclear Regulatory Commission's (NRC's) budget authority is aggregated into the major categories of salaries and benefits, contract support, and travel. Salaries and benefits are estimated based upon full-time equivalent (FTE), pay rates, pay raise assumptions, and effective pay period for pay raise. Benefits cost include the Government's contributions for retirement, health benefits, life insurance, Medicare, Social Security, and the Thrift Savings Plan. Contract support consists of obligations for commercial contracts, interagency agreements, grants, and other nontravel services such as rent and utility payments. Travel costs consist primarily of the expenses for nuclear reactor inspection trips.

Budget Authority by Function (Dollars In Millions)				
	FY 2011 Enacted	FY 2012 Enacted	FY 2013 Request	Changes from FY 2012
Salaries and Expenses (S&E)				
Salaries and Benefits	593.4	607.3	594.0	(13.3)
Contract Support	420.4	391.2	418.7	27.5
Travel	29.4	28.7	29.5	0.8
Total (S&E)	$1,043.2	$1,027.2	$1,042.2	$15.0
Office of the Inspector General (OIG)				
Salaries and Benefits	9.5	9.6	9.6	0.0
Contract Support	1.2	1.0	1.1	0.1
Travel	0.2	0.2	0.2	0.0
Total (OIG)	$10.9	$10.9	$11.0	$0.2
Total NRC Appropriation				
Salaries and Benefits	602.8	616.9	603.6	(13.3)
Contract Support	421.6	392.3	419.9	27.6
Travel	29.6	28.9	29.7	0.8
Total (NRC)	$1,054.1	$1,038.1	$1,053.2	$15.1

Numbers may not add due to rounding.

APPENDIX II
CORPORATE
SUPPORT

APPENDIX II: CORPORATE SUPPORT

APPENDIX II: CORPORATE SUPPORT

The Fiscal Year (FY) 2013 Congressional Budget Justification identifies the infrastructure and support costs for the U.S. Nuclear Regulatory Commission (NRC) and distributes them to programs as a portion of the total program cost. The allocation methodology is consistent with the methodology used for preparing the agency's financial statements. The business line tables present the associated infrastructure and support funding included in the programmatic funding to provide the full cost of each business line.

Corporate Support by Business Line (Dollars in Millions)						
	FY 2012 Enacted		FY 2013 Request		Delta FY 2013–FY 2012	
Business Line	$M	FTE	$M	FTE	$M	FTE
Operating Reactors	185.4	408.3	190.3	413.1	4.9	4.8
New Reactors	84.1	185.2	87.2	189.3	3.1	4.0
Nuclear Reactor Safety	**$269.4**	593.6	**$277.5**	602.4	**$8.0**	8.8
Fuel Facilities	20.4	44.9	20.6	44.7	0.2	(0.2)
Nuclear Materials Users	29.8	65.7	30.2	65.5	0.3	(0.2)
Spent Fuel Storage and Transportation	14.6	32.2	15.6	33.9	1.0	1.7
Decommissioning and Low-Level Waste	13.3	29.3	13.4	29.0	0.1	(0.3)
High-Level Waste Repository	0.0	0.0	0.0	0.0	0.0	0.0
Nuclear Materials and Waste Safety	**$78.1**	172.0	**$79.7**	173.1	**$1.6**	1.1
Total Corporate Support Allocation	**$347.5**	765.6	**$357.2**	775.5	**$9.7**	9.9

Numbers may not add due to rounding.

The agency's infrastructure and support involve centrally managed activities that are necessary for the staff and agency programs to achieve goals more efficiently and effectively. These activities include administrative services, financial management, generic homeland security, human resource management, information management (IM), information technology (IT), outreach, and policy support. The workload, resource changes from the FY 2012 enacted budget, and significant accomplishments for the product lines listed above are described in the following pages. The outputs of the product lines under Corporate Support contribute to the NRC Safety and Security Performance Measures and their contribution to the achievement of its strategic outcomes. The above table provides a cost breakdown of infrastructure and support by program.

APPENDIX II: CORPORATE SUPPORT

Corporate Support Budget Authority and Full-Time Equivalents by Product Line
(Dollars in Millions)

Product Line	FY 2012 Enacted		FY 2013 Request		Delta FY 2013–FY 2012	
	$M	FTE	$M	FTE	$M	FTE
Administrative Services	105.7	106.4	122.1	105.2	16.3	(1.2)
Financial Management	46.1	167.1	44.8	172.2	(1.4)	5.1
Generic HLS	0.9	1.3	0.0	0.0	(0.9)	(1.3)
Human Resource Management	29.4	82.8	29.7	84.9	0.3	2.2
Information Management	24.8	82.8	27.7	89.6	2.9	6.8
Information Technology	82.2	122.8	86.3	127.6	4.1	4.8
Outreach	19.8	19.3	9.5	19.3	(10.3)	(0.0)
Policy Support	36.7	183.1	35.3	176.7	(1.4)	(6.5)
Travel	1.9	0.0	2.0	0.0	0.0	0.0
Total	$347.5	765.6	$357.2	775.5	$9.7	9.9

Numbers may not add due to rounding.

ADMINISTRATIVE SERVICES

The Administrative Services budget provides resources for rent and utilities for Headquarters (HQ), regional, and Technical Training Center space; corporate rulemaking; IT systems that support security, space planning, rulemaking, facilities management, and administrative services for the agency; facilities management costs including systems and office furniture, property management, labor services, custodial services, operation and maintenance services, and building alterations; support services including shuttles, transit subsidies, supplies, and multimedia services; physical and personal security services including security equipment and investigations, drug testing, and guard services; and support and guard services in the regions.

Changes from FY 2012 Enacted Budget

In FY 2013, resources increase for rent, utilities, and security costs associated with the first full year of occupancy at the Three White Flint North Building and Region I's new location, as well as inflationary costs associated with rent, utilities, and security at HQ and the regions.

Significant Accomplishments in FY 2011

In support of Executive Order 13514, "Federal Leadership in Environmental, Energy, and Economic Performance", the NRC installed energy management system equipment that resulted in efficiencies in electrical consumption and has continued efforts in support of greening the Government by installing by installing motion-activated lighting and plumbing fixtures. In addition, for the second consecutive year, the NRC was recognized for outstanding achievement in recycling by Montgomery County, MD.

To improve employee security at the White Flint Complex (WFC), the NRC (1) expanded the lobby of the government-owned One White Flint North Building to provide better visitor management and a more secure area to screen visitors and their packages, (2) installed access control turnstiles with electronic badge authentication, and (3) closed the pedestrian entrance to visitors entering the Two White Flint North Building. In addition, the NRC repaved the WFC plaza in an effort to improve pedestrian safety.

FINANCIAL MANAGEMENT

In order to achieve the effective and efficient use of the agency's financial resources, the FY 2013 Financial Management request supports the modernization and operation of the agency's financial systems, acquisition of goods and services, budget development and execution, agency financial services, accounting and reporting activities, administration of a robust internal control program, and strategic and performance planning.

Resources for financial systems modernization will be used to provide steady-state operational support for the new core financial system, Financial Accounting and Integrated Management Information System (FAIMIS) and continue implementation of an enterprisewide acquisition system that will be integrated with the agency's core financial system.

Changes From FY 2012 Enacted Budget

In FY 2013, resources reflect a reduction to IT and Performance Improvement resources for Lean Six Sigma business process improvement projects.

Significant Accomplishments in FY 2011

The NRC has taken a number of actions to improve financial management within the agency during FY 2011. Significant accomplishments in this area include progress towards the modernization of financial systems, augmentation of the agency's contracting and procurement practices, enhancements to the Budget Formulation System, implementation of budget execution and funds utilization new processes, receipt of an unqualified opinion on the FY 2010 Financial Statements Audit, and continued improvement in the agency's business processes.

The NRC's systems modernization effort included the deployment of FAIMIS on October 1, 2010, throughout the agency. FAIMIS replaced five core financial systems with a single Web-based commercial-off-the-shelf software system. Standardized financial reports were developed that are centralized, timely, flexible, complete, and transparent to be used consistently across the agency to eliminate the need for custom reporting solutions.

In addition, the NRC implemented an upgrade to the Time and Labor (T&L) System, Human Resources Management System (HRMS). The upgrade provides a modern, Web-enabled version of the existing PeopleSoft T&L software. While this is an upgrade in versions, there are significant differences between the two versions that make the effort similar to a new implementation. The upgraded system provides increased security, is employee managed, paperless, and allows for electronic workflow and electronic signature approval. The new system was implemented in October 2011.

Due to continued enhancements to the agency's financial management processes, the NRC once again achieved operational excellence in FY 2011. The NRC received an unqualified audit opinion for the FY 2011 Financial Statements with no material weaknesses, significant deficiencies, or instances of noncompliance with laws and regulations noted. The NRC completed all other FY 2011 external reporting submissions to U.S. Department of the Treasury and Office of Management and Budget (OMB) on time. In addition, the 2011 Final Fee Rule was published on schedule. Additionally, for the tenth consecutive time, the NRC received the Certificate of Excellence in Accountability Reporting award from the Association of Government Accountants.

The agency performed all aspects of contract management necessary to ensure that the agency obtains goods and services in an efficient and effective manner consistent with mission needs and sound business practices. This includes contract negotiation, award, administration and closeout, grants award and administration, and administration of the NRC Purchase Card Program and the Agency Acquisition Certification and Training Program. The agency also provided oversight for commercial contracts, grants, and interagency agreements, including those with U.S. Department of Energy (DOE) laboratories. During FY 2011, the agency exceeded OMB's goals for contract savings and for reductions in high-risk contracts, achieved 100 percent FAC-COTR certification of its contracting officers' technical representatives, initiated an Acquisition Professional Development Program to support the training and development of entry-level contracting specialists, developed a Vendor Communications Plan, and implemented strategic sourcing processes and expanded use of enterprisewide contracts.

The NRC continued to make progress in implementing a 21st-Century Strategic Acquisition Program. The agency performed an indepth analysis of all procurement activity for the period FY 2008–FY2010. Information from this analysis is being utilized by a pilot Portfolio Council, which will manage the agency's strategy for purchasing a specific line of related products and services. The agency is also in the process of planning the implementation and life-cycle activities for an acquisition system module that will be integrated with the agency's core financial system. The system will provide a single acquisition portal and document generator with defined workflow, business rules, and enhanced reporting capability. A data warehouse of the NRC's DOE laboratory and interagency agreements, along with their critical supporting documentation, has been established in anticipation of the data migration into the acquisition system. During FY 2011, the NRC performed a process improvement on the agency's enterprisewide contracts to improve the efficiency of the process and timeliness of contracted services and started the restructuring of the NRC performance measures and metrics.

NRC staff successfully completed seven Business Process Improvement (BPI) projects and started seven others, including projects that will reduce agency overhead, as the result of increased efficiency and effectiveness. In addition, reliance on contractors for process improvement has continued to diminish as the expertise of the agency's BPI team has continued to increase. The NRC's BPI team regularly interacts with the Federal Improvement team for the purpose of sharing BPI best practices with the 120 members who represent 30 different Federal improvement organizations. Further, the NRC performed a comprehensive review of agency overhead functions (e.g., administrative services, human capital, financial management, including contract management, information management and information technology), to identify effective, efficient and cost-conscious business solutions and eliminate duplicative processes and functions.

GENERIC HOMELAND SECURITY

There are no resources in the Generic Homeland Security budget in FY 2013 as the requirements to implement Homeland Security Presidential Directive – 12 will be fully implemented by FY 2013, and any resources supporting maintenance of security equipment and physical access control systems are budgeted with other recurring costs in Administrative Services.

HUMAN RESOURCE MANAGEMENT

In FY 2013, resources provide for professional development training including leadership training; recruitment and staffing activities; work-life services; including employee counseling; employee and labor relations; and agencywide policy development and strategic workforce planning. In addition, resources provide for Permanent Change of Station Program activities, including resident inspector moves and new agency hires, as well as oversight of the Open Collaborative Work Environment (differing professional opinions, nonconcurrence process, and open door policy), and Internal Safety Culture Program activities.

Changes from FY 2012 Enacted Budget

There are no significant changes from the FY 2012 enacted budget.

Significant Accomplishments in FY 2011

For several years, the NRC experienced significant growth resulting from an increased interest in nuclear power. Currently, the NRC's staff levels have stabilized and the agency is not expected to grow further over the next several years. The NRC is adjusting its human capital strategies to ensure continued success. The NRC is strategically focusing on not only replacing employees who depart if necessary but also fine-tuning available skill sets to meet future mission needs. The agency has already taken steps to meet this challenge. The NRC has restricted external hiring to only those most critical skill sets, while still emphasizing governmentwide programs such as hiring of the disabled and veterans. The agency is maximizing internal movement to meet changing resource needs. With that objective in mind, the NRC hosted an internal career fair earlier this year, which gave staff an opportunity to explore career options involving rotations and reassignments within the agency. These and other changes are making the agency more streamlined, efficient and effective.

The agency's training and development programs are also adapting to the changing needs of the agency staff. By focusing on a competency-based approach to training, the NRC is ensuring a line-of-sight alignment between employees' learning experiences and the agency's mission. The agency is exploring and exploiting training technologies such as online and distance learning to deliver quality learning interventions at best cost, when and where they are needed. The agency is evolving its learning and development programs to support the needs of the next generation of regulatory experts.

Although the agency's forward focus is on optimizing the organization, the NRC is mindful of the high number of senior experts and managers who are becoming eligible to retire. The NRC has in place a variety of human capital strategies to maintain and bolster knowledge and skills during a period when many experienced staff members are becoming eligible to retire, and current and new NRC employees need the benefit of their knowledge. The agency continues to expand and enhance its Knowledge Management Program by actively capturing lessons learned from subject matter experts, improving access to lessons learned and training programs, and aggressively building an agencywide knowledge center.

The NRC is proud to be ranked as one of the best places to work in the Federal Government according to Federal Human Capital Survey results. The agency excels in areas such as matching employees' skills to the agency's mission, strategic management, effective leadership, performance-based advancements, training and development, support for diversity, and work-life balance. Clearly, these are important areas for any agency looking to attract and retain talent. The NRC realizes that the success of the agency depends on the talent and commitment of its employees. Therefore, the NRC is striving to create a workplace rich in work-life balance where employees are engaged in meaningful and challenging work.

INFORMATION MANAGEMENT

The IM program develops and implements the framework and technologies for managing and protecting information to ensure it is available to support a stable and predictable regulatory environment. In FY 2013, IM resources will provide document and records management services such as the operation of the Public Document Room; electronic document intake, profiling, indexing, and retrieval; modernization of internal and external Web sites; and compliance with the Freedom of Information Act (FOIA) and the Privacy Act.

Information security activities support secure communications and information security, policy and procedures, maintenance/services and supplies, classification management, and management of Sensitive Unclassified Nonsafeguards Information. FY 2013 resources will fund implementation of a new Governmentwide policy on Controlled Unclassified Information (CUI).

Central management of the agency's subscriptions to technical journals and databases, online codes and standards, and electronic newsletters and journals supports the scientific and research work of the agency staff, as well as the regulatory mission of the agency. Electronic newsletters are an integral component of communication within the energy industry, and these subscriptions ensure that the Commission, management, and staff maintain currency with industry developments, political decisions, and stakeholder concerns. Subscriptions to industry codes and standards are necessary to support the staff's determinations of compliance with Commission regulations. The codes and standards are cited in the regulations, and staff members require access to cited codes and standards to conduct the necessary inspections and reviews to determine compliance with NRC requirements.

Changes From FY 2012 Enacted Budget

In FY 2013, resources increase to support automation of agency business processes in the upgraded Agencywide Documents Access and Management System (ADAMS) environment, implementation of CUI policy, the redesign and reorganization of the agency's intranet sites, and centralization of agency Web support activities.

Significant Accomplishments in FY 2011

Effective IM ensures needed information is available to the staff to help support predictable regulatory programs and policies. It also allows the NRC to meet its openness objective related to informing and involving stakeholders in the regulatory process by providing timely access to accurate agency information. Technology improvements completed in FY 2011 included modernizing ADAMS to ensure staff and stakeholders can readily access needed information; deploying improved public search capabilities, such as a single search of the NRC public Web site that provides stakeholders with more comprehensive search results; and redesigning and modernizing the NRC's public Web site to help provide users with better organized and more easily navigable information. During FY 2011, stakeholders were able to work directly with a professional librarian to retrieve information available through the agency's Public Document Room, and key information was promptly disseminated to public stakeholders through timely public meeting notices, FOIA responses, and documents made publicly available through ADAMS. The agency also completed deployment of the Safeguards Information Local Area Network and Electronic Safe System.

INFORMATION TECHNOLOGY

In FY 2013, resources will fund the NRC's IT infrastructure, end-user support services for IT applications, database and application support for agency systems, and configuration management and IT project management support. Funded programs include Capital Planning and Investment Control (CPIC) processes, IT strategic management and enterprise architecture planning, and agencywide IT procurement management.

The budget will fund the following ongoing activities:

> IT infrastructure end-user support services, telecommunications services, network and production operations, and central management of all desktop, laptop, and network resources and services at HQ, regional offices, and resident inspector sites. Resources support the Network Operations Center, Customer Support Center, the Consolidated Testing Facility, and seat management and desktop support for over 5,000 desktop workstations and the supporting infrastructure. Also included are the managed public key infrastructure and production operations support, including systems administration and data center operations.

> Identification of the best technologies to fill gaps associated with strategic goals such as "Working from Anywhere" and "Working with Anyone," and identifying, testing, and piloting new technology needed to support specific agency business needs. Recent examples include technologies to support the NRC's Open Government flagship initiative such as enhancing stakeholder engagement using innovative and cost-effective collaboration technologies, defining common strategies to support mobile and universal access, and consolidating systems into enterprise solutions.

> The NRC's legacy system modernization/transformation program. Resources will be used to support an effective CPIC Program, for enterprisewide configuration management, and for maintenance and operational support of approximately 120 application systems. In addition, resources will support project management, business analysis, and applications development for office-specific and enterprise-wide applications.

> Compliance with the Federal Information Security Management Act (FISMA), IT security policy, standards, training, cyber situational awareness and response, and security authorization of all NRC IT systems. Resources support utilization of distinctive IT security tools and expertise to provide a robust cyber program for the protection of NRC cyber assets. Efforts support infrastructure operations, including system authorization activities, penetration testing and system scanning, development of policies and standards, and development and delivery of computer security training and awareness. Also employed are automated forensic software and hardware products used in responding to security incidents. The cyber security experts also review new technologies and work with system owners to ensure those technologies are implemented in a way that is safe and meets federally mandated and NRC-defined security requirements.

> Cyber Situational Awareness Program for penetration testing, vulnerability and threat assessments, real-time monitoring, visibility and reporting, and computer security incident response, along with providing insight into the security impact that new technologies will have on the NRC infrastructure and enable continuous cyber security reporting.

> Reduction of the NRC's data center footprint. Efforts include leveraging a combination of strategies to lower energy consumption and operations costs through increased use of cloud computing alternatives, managing the NRC's application system modernization initiatives, strengthening server and desktop virtualization,

and setting into operation other green IT technologies across the enterprise. As a part of the NRC HQ building, the NRC will build an energy-efficient modern data center that uses green technologies in space, design, power, heating, ventilation, and cooling to support energy-efficient 24/7 data center operations.

Changes From FY 2012 Enacted Budget

Resources increase due to fixed infrastructure costs, enhancement of the IT security program, and support for centralization of IT infrastructure and application support activities.

Significant Accomplishments in FY 2011

Effective IT infrastructure ensures that the NRC has a reliable and responsive foundation of technology to support business needs and agency operations to advance the NRC mission. A major achievement in this area was the award of the new Information Technology Infrastructure and Support Services contract, which will provide key IT services across the enterprise. Other key successes included the transition of telecommunications services from FTS2001 to Networx and implementation of the Federal Government mandate for Trusted Internet Connection. Also during FY 2011, the agency enabled network access through the use of Personal Identity Verification cards; expanded use of the Safeguards Information Local Area Network and Electronic Safe System to HQ satellite offices, regional offices, and all resident inspector sites to allow secure network access to safeguards information data; and replatformed and redesigned the protected Web server used to securely communicate security incidents that occur at licensee locations.

The NRC has developed a plan to map strategic programs and business objectives to the agency security architecture to provide a prioritized blueprint for secure IT capability. The NRC implemented an Automated Plan of Action and Milestone process that uses an automated tool to improve quality assurance and timely reporting by system owners.

Another primary focus area is service, a key component of operational excellence across the agency. In a continuing effort to evaluate the effectiveness of its IT/IM services, the NRC solicited feedback from employees on its IT/IM program by adding questions on this topic to the employee viewpoint survey conducted in FY 2011. The agency is also conducting an independent validation and verification of its IT/IM services to assess the costs of existing services and to establish clear service expectations. The NRC has also conducted a facilitated process to update its IT/IM Strategic Plan in coordination with ongoing efforts to update the NRC Strategic Plan. Also contributing to planning and budget formulation is the IT/IM Roadmap that provides a view of current IT/IM capabilities and agency transition plans through 2013. The procurement to establish a new enterprisewide contract for maintenance, operation, and modernization of agency IT systems was initiated in FY 2011.

OUTREACH

In FY 2013, resources provide for outreach activities, which include maintaining a positive, discrimination-free work environment; advocating for contracts with small businesses; and continuing efforts to implement the NRC's Outreach and Compliance Coordination Program, in accordance with applicable Federal civil rights statutes and NRC regulations.

Resources also provide $4.7 million for the grants to universities/curriculum development program.

Resources also support hosting of the annual Regulatory Information Conference (RIC) with the nuclear industry to discuss safety and regulatory issues of mutual interest. The objective of the RIC is to provide a communication forum for senior NRC and industry management regarding current and future safety initiatives and regulatory issues.

Changes from FY 2012 Enacted Budget

In FY 2013, resources decrease by $10.0 million as compared with the enacted FY 2012 amount.

Outreach Significant Accomplishments In FY 2011

SIGNIFICANT ACCOMPLISHMENTS IN FY 2011

The Small Business Program (SBP) continued to host the NRC Quarterly Business Seminars. These seminars introduce the agency, its mission, and business opportunities, and educate the business community about the NRC's cultural and technical program environment. The seminar series provided information and guidance to more than 200 participants in the second quarter and is expected to reach over 1,000 participants during the fiscal year through in-person, Webstreaming, and Webinar participation. The SBP continued to implement strategies for the "Helmets to Business" initiative to reach out to the veteran business community to promote contracting and partnership opportunities. Based on contract awards to date, the agency is increasing contracts awarded to Service-Disabled Veteran-Owned Small Businesses.

In FY 2011, the NRC conducted 129 mandatory preaward compliance reviews for financial assistance awards and provided technical assistance to the applicants and recipients during the preaward compliance review process. Technical assistance was provided to NRC offices to enhance diversity management strategies designed to improve individual and organizational performance in a positive work environment. Technical assistance was also provided to NRC offices on compliance with limited English proficiency regulations and requirements imposed under disability legislation. The agency processed informal and formal complaints, completed investigations, and conducted mediations. The Facilitated Mentoring Program continued to enhance knowledge transfer and the career progression of employees. Additionally, the NRC conducted a mentoring orientation program for pairs and individual mentees and provided individual counseling sessions to mentees to define career goals as well as to identify mentors who could provide mentees with information regarding current program activities and future program directions consistent with these career goals.

There has been and continues to be a critical shortage of personnel in the nuclear sector as the current workforce retires and normal attrition occurs. The NRC has grant programs to provide grants to educational institutions in the areas of curriculum development, faculty development, fellowships, and scholarships to 4-year institutions and scholarships to trade schools and community colleges. The agency has provided over 129 grants to educational institutions in 33 States. These grants have assisted over 100 faculty members and well over 1,000 students involved in nuclear engineering, health physics, radiochemistry, and related disciplines. These grants assist in expanding the workforce in nuclear safety and nuclear-related disciplines and the development of the next-generation nuclear workforce. The areas of focus for the grants are nuclear engineering, health physics, radiochemistry, and other related areas that benefit the nuclear sector.

POLICY SUPPORT

Resources in FY 2013 will provide for additional policy and adjudicatory support to the Commission. Specifically, the budget provides resources for the following:

> Agency policy formulation and guidance.

> Legal advice and adjudicatory review to the Commission.

> Independent evaluations of agency programs and implementation of Commission policy directives.

> Interaction with the Executive Branch on matters of international nuclear safety and security issues and developments.

> Work with the International Atomic Energy Agency, the Nuclear Energy Agency, and other international partners.

> Advice and assistance to the Commission on congressional and protocol issues and public affairs activities leading to openness and increased public confidence.

> Management and oversight of agency programs.

Changes from FY 2012 Enacted Budget

In FY 2013, resources decrease primarily due to the elimination of the Commission Adjudicatory Technical Support Program.

CORPORATE SUPPORT OUTPUT MEASURES

Financial Management

OMB-Directed Acquisition Reform Initiative Measure. Percent of Eligible Service Contracting Dollars (Contracts Over $25,000) that use Performance-Based Contracting Techniques During the Fiscal Year.					
	FY 2008	FY 2009	FY 2010	FY 2011	FY 2012	FY 2013
Target:	Not less than 65%	Not less than 65%	Not less than 65%	Not less than 65%	Not less than 65%	Not less than 65%
Actual:	78%	89%	79%	69%		

OMB-Directed Acquisition Reform Initiative Measure - Percent of Required Synopses for Acquisitions that are Posted on the Governmentwide Point-of-Entry Website (www.FedBizOpps.gov) During the Fiscal Year*					
	FY 2008	FY 2009	FY 2010	FY 2011	FY 2012	FY 2013
Target:	100% of all required synopses	100% of all required synopses	100% of all required synopses	100% of all required synopses	100% of all required synopses	100% of all required synopses
Actual:	100%	100%	100%	100%		

*Percent of required synopses for acquisitions that are posted on the governmentwide point-of-entry Website (www.FedBizOpps.gov) during the FY. Synopses for acquisitions are those valued at over $25,000 for which widespread notice is required, including all associated solicitations except for acquisitions covered by an exemption in the Federal Acquisition Regulations.

OMB Directed Acquisition Reform Initiative Measure—Number Of Business Case Analyses.*					
	FY 2008	FY 2009	FY 2010	FY 2011	FY 2012	FY 2013
Target:	3 business case analyses.	3 business case analyses.**	3 business case analyses. **	3 business case analyses. **	Measure deleted	Measure deleted
Actual:	3	1	0	0		

*Competitive Sourcing FY 2004. Number of business case analyses (BCA) performed on commercial activities listed on the approved FAIR Act inventory and conducted in accordance with Agency competitive sourcing plan. (Measure Revised in FY 2004.)

**During FY 2009, one reverse business case analysis was completed. Notice was provided to OMB that the agency competitive sourcing plan was revised to delete the requirement to perform a minimum of 3 BCAs annually. The target will remain at 3 for FY 2010 and FY2011 as required, but the agency may not perform any additional business case analysis. Additional guidance from the current administration is anticipated to clarify the future direction of the competitive sourcing program. The target may be revised once that clarification is obtained. Notification to OMB of NRC's planned change in strategy in using BCA's was issued on September 8, 2009.

Meet Statutory Fee Collection Requirement						
	FY 2008	FY 2009	FY 2010	FY 2011	FY 2012	FY 2013
Target:	Achieve approximately 100% actual collections when compared with projected collections. Maintain past due accounts receivable at 1% or less of annual billings for the fiscal year.	Achieve approximately 100% actual collections when compared with projected collections. Maintain past due accounts receivable at 1% or less of annual billings for the fiscal year.	Achieve approximately 100% actual collections when compared with projected collections. Maintain past due accounts receivable at 1% or less of annual billings for the fiscal year.	Achieve approximately 100% actual collections when compared with projected collections. Maintain past due accounts receivable at 1% or less of annual billings for the fiscal year.	Achieve approximately 100% actual collections when compared with projected collections. Maintain past due accounts receivable at 1% or less of annual billings for the fiscal year.	Achieve approximately 100% collections when compared with projected collections. Maintain past due accounts receivable at 1% or less of annual billings for the fiscal year.
Actual:	98% collected. Maintained past due amounts receivable at less than 1% of annual billings.	98% collected. Maintained past due amounts receivable at less than 1% of annual billings.	Target met	99.5% collected. Past due amounts receivable were 1.34% of annual billings.		

Percentage of Nonsalary Payments Made Electronically and Accurately Within Established Schedule						
	FY 2008	FY 2009	FY 2010	FY 2011	FY 2012	FY 2013
Target:	98%	98%	98%	98%	98%	98%
Actual:	99%	96%	98%	98%		

Human Resource Management

Percent of Actual FTE Utilization						
	FY 2008	FY 2009	FY 2010	FY 2011	FY 2012	FY 2013
Target:	85%	85%	85%	85%	85%	85%
Actual:	82%	87%	89%	91%		

Information Management

Information Dissemination Timeliness—Meets Agency Targets for Key Information Dissemination Channels, Including Public Meeting Notices, Freedom ff Information Act*						
	FY 2008	FY 2009	FY 2010	FY 2011	FY 2012	FY 2013
Target:	New measure in FY 2009	Timeliness targets met for FOIA responses, public meeting notices, and NRC documents made publicly available [1]	Meet 3 out of 4 targets.	Meet 3 out of 4 targets.	Meet 3 out of 4 targets.	Meet 3 out of 4 targets.
Actual:		86%	4 out of 4	4 out of 4		

*Targets: (1) Percent of the time NRC responds to FOIA requests within 20 working days (75%), (2) percentage of category 1,2, and 3 meetings on regulatory issues for which NRC posted a meeting notice on the public meeting notice Web site at least 10 days in advance of the meeting (90%), (3) percent of nonsensitive, unclassified regulatory documents generated by the NRC and sent to the agency's Document Processing Center that are released to the public by the 6th working day after the date of the document (90%), (4) percent of nonsensitive, unclassified regulatory documents received by the NRC that are released to the public by the 6th working day after the document is added to the ADAMS main library (90%).

Public Score for Information Access–The NRC Score on the Annual American Customer Satisfaction Index for Federal Web Sites						
	FY 2008	FY 2009	FY 2010	FY 2011	FY 2012	FY 2013
Target:	New measure in FY 2013				TBD; target to be baselined in FY 2012.	73
Actual:						

Information Technology

Percent of the Time that Key IT Infrastructure Services are Available						
	FY 2008	FY 2009	FY 2010	FY 2011	FY 2012	FY 2013
Target:	New measure in FY 2009	99.50%	99.50%*	99.50%*	99.50%*	Measure replaced with Reduced Passwords and/or Sign-on measure.
Actual:		100%	99.90%	99.90%		

This measure is calculated based on statistics gathered each month from a network monitoring tool that constantly monitors the availability status of key infrastructure components. It shows the amount of time, in minutes, that all (any) infrastructure components were unavailable. That information is then used to calculate the overall availability percentage based on number of working days in each month (the total hours of operation) and the number of people supported by each component.

*Target previously reported as 100% was in error.

IT Security Risk Management—Percent of Operational Applications and General Support Systems that have Met NRC's Annual Risk Management Activities Requirements in Accordance with Guidance from the CIO*

	FY 2008	FY 2009	FY 2010	FY 2011	FY 2012	FY 2013
Target:	New measure in FY 2010.		95%	95%	95%	Measure to be replaced with Cyber Security Program Effectiveness measure.
Actual:			96%	97%		

*This measure replaced the output measure "Systems Certification and Accreditation-percent of major applications and general support that have been certified and accredited" from the FY 2011 budget. The measure includes Certification and Accreditation along with other risk management activities.

IT Investment Management—Average Score on a Scale Of 1–10 aor all NRC IT Investments on the OMB IT Dashboard*

	FY 2008	FY 2009	FY 2010	FY 2011	FY 2012	FY 2013
Target:	New measure in FY 2010.		>7.5	> 7.5	> 7.0	**Green Range
Actual:			6.38	7.53		

This measure replaces the output measure OMB Exhibit 300 Score - percent of major IT investments that are rated as 'acceptable' based on OMB's evaluation of NRC's Exhibit 300 submittal" from the FY 2011 budget. The OMB Exhibit 300 Score measure has been replaced by the IT Dashboard Score.

** "TBD pending OMB release of revised IT Dashboard."

Reduced Passwords and/or Sign-On – Percent of NRC-Controlled Systems Requiring User Authentication That are Implemented to use the NRC LAN Account or NRC Personal Identity Verification (PIV) Card as the Means to Control User Access*

	FY 2008	FY 2009	FY 2010	FY 2011	FY 2012	FY 2013
Target:	New measure in FY 2013				TBD; measure to be baselined in FY 2012.	Preliminary target to be established.
Actual:						

*This measure replaces the output measure "Percent of the time that key IT infrastructure services are available" from the FY 2012 budget.

Cyber Security Program Effectiveness—Rating ff the NRC's Cyber Security Program Effectiveness Based Upon the Annual IG FISMA Audit*

	FY 2008	FY 2009	FY 2010	FY 2011	FY 2012	FY 2013
Target:	New measure in FY 2013.					Satisfactory in all areas.
Actual:						

*This measure replaces the output measure "IT Security Risk Management- Percent of operational applications and general support systems that have met NRC's annual risk management activities requirements in accordance with guidance from the CIO" from the FY 2011 budget.

APPENDIX III
REIMBURSABLE WORK

The U.S. Nuclear Regulatory Commission (NRC) performs services for other Federal agencies and non-Federal organizations on a reimbursable basis. Reimbursable work performed by the NRC is financed with funds of the ordering organization and represents additional funding in excess of the NRC's directly appropriated funds.

Summary of Reimbursable Work (New Budget Authority in Thousands of Dollars)	FY 2011 (Actual)	FY 2012 (Projection)	FY 2013 (Projection)
Technical Assistance to Other Federal Agencies			
CMRR/UPF Support (DOD)	5	0	0
Employee Detail to Domestic Nuclear Detection Office (DHS)	184	174	174
Employee Detail to National Counterterrorism Center (NCTC)	189	81	162
Fuel Cycle Research and Development (DOE)	0	500	500
Gerald R. Ford Class Aircraft Carrier Safety Review (DOE)	45	830	2,758
Joint Funding of ICRP Activities (EPA)	50	25	25
Mars Science Laboratory Mission (NASA)	20	60	0
Navy Reviews (U.S. Navy)	12	12	12
Next Generation Nuclear Plant (NGNP) Cooperative Activities (DOE)	4,500	2,800	2,500
Review/Approval of Selected Foreign Certificates for Packages (Casks) (DOE)	100	100	100
Review of Alternate Transportation Security Protocol (DOE)	100	0	0
Route Reviews (DOE)	0	0	0
Waste Actions for Hanford (DOE)	265	100	100
Waste Review for West Valley (DOE)	0	0	0
Workshop on Ash-Fall Hazards (USGS)	1	0	0
International Assistance			
International Invitational Travel (IAEA & various foreign governments and international organizations)	150	150	150
Invitational Travel - American Institute in Taiwan	0	20	20
Nuclear Safety Initiatives for the New Independent States (USAID)	750	0	0
Cooperative Research			
Environmentally Assisted Fatigue Effects (EPRI)	0	200	0
Foreign Cooperative Research Agreements (Multiple)	2,054	1,675	1,675
Security Related Activities			
Criminal History Program (Licensees)	1,667	2,086	2,148
Information Access Authorization Program (Licensees)	615	850	880
Material Access Authorization Program (Licensees)	0	0	0
Totals	**$10,707**	**$9,663**	**$11,204**

APPENDIX IV
AGENCY FEE RECOVERY

Assuming a full appropriation of the Fiscal Year 2013 requested budget, the projected inpact on fees is shown below.

Agency Fee Recovery (Dollars in Millions)		
	FY 2012 Proposed Fee Rule[1]	FY 2013 Projection[2]
Total Appropriation[3]	$1,038.1	$1,053.2
Less Non-Fee Items[4]	(27.5)	(25.7)
Base	1,010.6	1,027.5
Fee Recovery Rate – 90% of Base	909.5	924.8
Billing & Carryover Adjustments[5]	(8.5)	0.4
Amount to be Recovered through Fees	$901.0	$925.2
Estimated Part 170 Fees	$371.4	$381.2
Percent of Total Recovered Amount	41.2%	41.2%
Estimated Part 171 Annual Fees	$529.6	$544.0
Percent of Total Recovered Amount	58.8%	58.8%
Total Net Appropriated	$128.6	$128.5

Numbers may not add due to rounding.
Note: As a fee based agency, reduction to agency base budget yields a 10% reduction in net budget authority for every dollar of those reductions.

1 The FY 2012 proposed fee rule is preliminary data and is currently not published in the Federal Register.
2 Assuming same rate as FY 2012 for adjustments and split between 10 CFR Parts 170 and 171.
3 Includes both Salaries and Expenses and Inspector General Appropriations.
4 Non Fee Items

Nuclear Waste Fund (NWF)	$0.0	$0.0
Waste Incidental to Reprocessing (WIR)[6,7]	0.8	1.4
Generic Homeland Security	26.7	24.3
Total Non-Fee Items	$27.5	$25.7

5 Includes estimated unpaid invoices and payments of prior year invoices.
6 Prior year Waste Incidental to Reprocessing (WIR) appropriations totaling $1.2 million will be allocated in FY 2012. No significant prior year WIR appropriations are expected to be available in FY 2013.
7 The NRC is meeting the legal requirement of section 3116 of PL 108-375 by requesting the FY 2013 WIR budget of $1,411,000 from the General Fund.

APPENDIX V
REPORT TO CONGRESS
ON DRUG TESTING

Congress and the U.S. Department of Health and Human Services (DHHS) initially approved the Nuclear Regulatory Commission's (NRC's) Drug Testing Program in August 1988, and the agency subsequently updated the program in November 1997. The program was revised again and received approval from DHHS on August 23, 2007. The NRC's drug testing requirements for the nuclear industry (licensees), as imposed by agency regulations, are separate and distinct from this program and are not covered by this report.

The NRC's Drug Testing Program under Executive Order (E.O.) 12564 includes random, applicant, voluntary, follow-up, reasonable suspicion, and accident-related drug testing. Testing was initiated for non-bargaining unit employees in November 1988 and for bargaining unit employees in December 1990, after an agreement was negotiated with the National Treasury Employees Union. On August 25, 2008, NRC's testing program was expanded to include all NRC sensitive positions as testing designated and thereby all employees became subject to random drug testing.

During Fiscal Year (FY) 2011, the NRC conducted approximately 2,252 tests of all types between October 1, 2010 and September 30, 2011. There were three positive drug test results (two for marijuana and one for cocaine). These individuals completed outpatient treatment programs and are subject to follow-up drug testing. In addition, one federal employee came forward to admit use of cocaine. This employee also completed an outpatient treatment program as well and is subject to follow-up drug testing.

The NRC also completed internal quality control reviews during the past year to ensure that the agency's program continues to be administered in a fair, confidential, and effective manner.

The NRC's drug testing program is based on the principles and guidance according to E.O. 12564, Public Law 100-71, DHHS guidelines, and Commission decisions.

ACRONYM
LIST

ACRONYM LIST

ACP. American Centrifuge Plant.

ADAMS. Agencywide Documents Access and Management System.

ADR. Alternative Dispute Resolution.

AEA. Atomic Energy Act, as amended.

AEC. Atomic Energy Commission.

AO. Abnormal Occurrence.

ASME. The American Society of Mechanical Engineers.

ASP. Accident Secquence Precursor.

B&W. Babcock and Wilcox.

BCA. Business Case Analysis.

C&A. Certification and Accreditation.

CIGIE. Council of the Inspectors General on Integrity and Efficiency.

CFR. Code *of Federal Regulations.*

COC. Certificate of Compliance.

COL. Combined License.

CPIC. Capital Planning and Investment Control.

DBT. Design-Basis Threat.

DC. Design Certification.

DHHS. U.S. Department of Health and Human Services.

DHS. U.S. Department of Homeland Security.

DLLW. Decommissioning and Low-Level Waste program.

DOE. U.S. Department of Energy.

DOT. U.S. Department of Transportation.

EA. Environmental Assessment.

EIS. Environmental Impact Statement.

ENS. Emergency Notification System.

e-OPF. Electronic Official Personnel Folder.

EPA. U.S. Environmental Protection Agency.

ESP. Early Site Permit.

EST. Extended Storage and Transportation.

FAIMIS. Financial Accounting and Integrated Management Information System.

FEMA. Federal Emergency Management Agency.

FICAM. Federal Identity, Credential, and Access Management.

FISMA. Federal Information Security Management Act.

FOF. Force-on-Force.

FOIA. Freedom of Information Act.

FTE. Full-Time Equivalent.

FY. Fiscal Year.

GE-Hitachi. General Electric-Hitachi.

GEIS. Generic Environmental Impact Statement.

GWd/MTU. Gigawat-days/metric ton uranium.

HAB. Hostile-Action-Based Emergency Preparedness Drill.

HLW. High-Level Waste.

HQ. Headquarters.

HSPD. Homeland Security Presidential Directive.

I&C. Instrumentation and Control.

IAEA. International Atomic Energy Agency.

IAM. Identity and Access Management.

ICAM. Identity, Credential, and Access Management.

ICRP. International Commission on Radiological Protection.

IM. Information Management.

IMPEP. Integrated Materials Performance Evaluation Program.

ISFSI. Independent Spent Fuel Storage Installation.

ISG. Interim Staff Guidance.

ISMP. Integrated Source Management Portfolio.

ISR. In Situ Recovery.

IT. Information Technology.

ITAAC. Inspections, Tests, Analyses, and Acceptance Criteria.

IV&V. Independent Verification and Validation.

KEPCO. Korea Electric Power Corporation.

LER. Licensee Event Report.

LES. Louisiana Energy Services.

LERSearch. Licensee Event Report Search System.

LLW. Low-Level Waste.

LVS. License Verification System.

MOX. Mixed Oxide.

NEA. Nuclear Energy Agency.

NFPA. National Fire Protection Association.

NFS. Nuclear Fuel Services, Inc.

NGNP. Next Generation Nuclear Plant.

NMED. Nuclear Material Events Database.

NMIP. Nuclear Materials Information Program.

NMMSS. Nuclear Materials Management and Safeguards System.

NMP. National Materials Program.

NRC. U.S. Nuclear Regulatory Commission.

NSTS. National Source Tracking System.

NUREG. Nuclear Regulatory Commission Regulations and other publications. NUREGs are regulatory guides and publications issued by the U.S. Nuclear Regulatory Commission.

NWF. Nuclear Waste Fund.

OE. Office of Enforcement.

OI. Office of Investigations.

OIG. Office of the Inspector General.

OMB. Office of Management and Budget.

PBPM. Planning, Budget, and Performance Management.

P.L. Public Law.

PSEG. Public Service Enterprise Group.

RIS. Regulatory Information Summary.

ROP. Reactor Oversight Process.

RTR. Research and Test Reactor.

S&E. Salaries and Expenses .

SAPHIRE. System Analysis Programs for Hands-on Integrated Reliability Evaluation.

SCOL. Subsequent Combined License.

SDP. Significance Determination Process.

SEIS. Supplemental Environmental Impact Statement.

SER. Safety Evaluation Report.

SGI. Safeguards Information.

SLES. Secure Local Area Network and Electronic Safe.

SMR. Small Modular Reactor.

SNM. Special Nuclear Materials.

USAID. U.S. Agency for International Development.

US-ABWR. U.S. Advanced Boiling-Water Reactor.

US-APWR. U.S. Advanced Pressurized-Water Reactor.

USEC. U.S. Enrichment Corporation.

US-EPR. U.S. Evolutionary Power Reactor.

US-ESBWR. US-Economic Simplified Boiling-Water Reactor.

VA. U.S. Department of Veterans Affairs.

WBL. Web-Based Licensing.

WIR. Waste Incidental to Reprocessing.

WVDP. West Valley Demonstration Project

AVAILABILITY OF REFERENCE MATERIALS
IN NRC PUBLICATIONS

NRC Reference Material

As of November 1999, you may electronically access NUREG-series publications and other NRC records at NRC's Public Electronic Reading Room at http://www.nrc.gov/reading-rm.html.
Publicly released records include, to name a few, NUREG-series publications; *Federal Register* notices; applicant, licensee, and vendor documents and correspondence; NRC correspondence and internal memoranda; bulletins and information notices; inspection and investigative reports; licensee event reports; and Commission papers and their attachments.

NRC publications in the NUREG series, NRC regulations, and *Title 10, Energy,* in the Code of *Federal Regulations* may also be purchased from one of these two sources.
1. The Superintendent of Documents
    U.S. Government Printing Office
    Mail Stop SSOP
    Washington, DC 20402-0001
    Internet: bookstore.gpo.gov
    Telephone: 202-512-1800
    Fax: 202-512-2250
2. The National Technical Information Service
    Springfield, VA 22161-0002
    www.ntis.gov
    1-800-553-6847 or, locally, 703-605-6000

A single copy of each NRC draft report for comment is available free, to the extent of supply, upon written request as follows:
Address: U.S. Nuclear Regulatory Commission
           Office of Administration
           Publications Branch
           Washington, DC 20555-0001
E-mail: DISTRIBUTION.SERVICES@NRC.GOV
Facsimile: 301-415-2289

Some publications in the NUREG series that are posted at NRC's Web site address http://www.nrc.gov/reading-rm/doc-collections/nuregs are updated periodically and may differ from the last printed version. Although references to material found on a Web site bear the date the material was accessed, the material available on the date cited may subsequently be removed from the site.

Non-NRC Reference Material

Documents available from public and special technical libraries include all open literature items, such as books, journal articles, and transactions, *Federal Register* notices, Federal and State legislation, and congressional reports. Such documents as theses, dissertations, foreign reports and translations, and non-NRC conference proceedings may be purchased from their sponsoring organization.

Copies of industry codes and standards used in a substantive manner in the NRC regulatory process are maintained at—
       The NRC Technical Library
       Two White Flint North
       11545 Rockville Pike
       Rockville, MD 20852-2738

These standards are available in the library for reference use by the public. Codes and standards are usually copyrighted and may be purchased from the originating organization or, if they are American National Standards, from—
       American National Standards Institute
       11 West 42nd Street
       New York, NY 10036-8002
       www.ansi.org
       212-642-4900

Legally binding regulatory requirements are stated only in laws; NRC regulations; licenses, including technical specifications; or orders, not in NUREG-series publications. The views expressed in contractor-prepared publications in this series are not necessarily those of the NRC.

The NUREG series comprises (1) technical and administrative reports and books prepared by the staff (NUREG-XXXX) or agency contractors (NUREG/CR-XXXX), (2) proceedings of conferences (NUREG/CP-XXXX), (3) reports resulting from international agreements (NUREG/IA-XXXX), (4) brochures (NUREG/BR-XXXX), and (5) compilations of legal decisions and orders of the Commission and Atomic and Safety Licensing Boards and of Directors' decisions under Section 2.206 of NRC's regulations (NUREG-0750).

United States Nuclear Regulatory Commission
Office of the Chief Financial Officer
NUREG–1100, Vol. 28
February 2012

www.ingramcontent.com/pod-product-compliance
Lightning Source LLC
Chambersburg PA
CBHW082036290526
45791CB00015B/2225